Climate of Lament

Climate of Lament

Reflections on Ecological Grief

Edited by
PHILIP MINGAY and
MICHAEL FERBER

Forewords by
Elizabeth A. Horvath
and *Forrest Inslee*

WIPF & STOCK · Eugene, Oregon

Wipf & Stock
An Imprint of Wipf and Stock Publishers
199 W. 8th Ave., Suite 3
Eugene, OR 97401

www.wipfandstock.com

PAPERBACK ISBN: 979-8-3852-3412-7
HARDCOVER ISBN: 979-8-3852-3413-4
EBOOK ISBN: 979-8-3852-3414-1

VERSION NUMBER 02/06/26

For all who lament truthfully and still choose hope.

Contents

CONTENTS

Foreword

It is with a deep sense of responsibility, a heartfelt measure of gratitude, and no little measure of humility that I write a foreword for this collection of poems and their reflective summaries that touch on the action and practice of lament. Dr. Ferber has told me that I catalyzed the experience that led to the inspiration for this volume, and he has written about that moment in the introduction to this volume, as will I here. It is somewhat ironic that this event was the origin, as I tend to be shy and reticent about displaying emotion in public. Still, the moment in question was one where the topic of discussion was so extraordinarily personal for me that I could not do anything but let it be emotional. It was a moment of honest lament, gratefully shared with others, and I am honored to recount it for this volume.

I have been teaching college undergraduates in various fields of biology since the spring of 1977, initially as a first-year graduate student. My career practicing the "art" of teaching was not one that I had envisioned for myself. In fact, I made it quite clear in my first semester as a graduate student that I did not want to teach and that I would never get in front of a classroom. Through some sly action on the part of one of my committee members, however, one afternoon, I found myself teaching an invertebrate zoology lab. Long story short, I loved it! Sharing my interests and seeing others get excited about them was truly exhilarating! That semester, I ended up teaching two lab sections and found fulfillment and joy in every moment of that experience. In January 1978, while still pursuing my master's degree, I accepted a job offer from my undergraduate institution, taking on the responsibility of preparing both lectures and labs. This part-time position evolved into a full-time career, which I now consider my calling.

At the beginning of my career, an Indigenous speaker from my area told me during the meet and greet after his lecture on Native American culture that my spirit animal was the wolf (my mother continues to instill this in me). We had only briefly interacted when he, rather abruptly, but seriously and profoundly, made that statement. I learned from him that many Native Americans deeply revere the wolf as "teacher, pathfinder"; his story about the wolf filled me with such wonder, and his knowledge of local plant and animal life revealed to me that there is much to learn, not only from textbooks but also from working in and with creation, and from knowledgeable people from different cultures. Three things became clear to me at that moment: why I was indeed doing what I never intended to do; why I want to teach in a field, or on a beach, or in a forest rather than in a classroom; and why I have always had such a strong affinity with/for wolves. I hope, over my years as a teacher, that I have honored my spirit animal. God works in mysterious ways; his wonders to perform! But, many of those "wonders" are indeed threatened, and that is a deeply anguishing thought.

As an associate professor of biology, my areas of interest center on life in the marine world, and I am happiest when tides are low and I can spend multiple hours in the intertidal zone. To open that world to my students is one of my greatest delights. While I am an invertebrate zoologist/ecologist, having worked with gorgonian corals for the last twenty-plus years, I also have had numerous opportunities to witness the largest of marine mammal species in a variety of contexts and to share those experiences and knowledge with my students. Sighting live marine mammal species, especially baleen whales and dolphins, is nothing short of breathtaking—it never gets old and is always a privilege, albeit sometimes rare, but always deeply emotional.

To comprehend the depth of my laments, you need to hear about the heights of my joys with the species I love. There are many "firsts" I could recount, from encounters with a giant Pacific octopus spending over an hour "tasting" me (and finding me a "friend"), to a gorilla who kept moving closer and closer, so as to hear me speaking quietly to him. From a gray whale rolling to one side to look me in the eye as I hung over the side of a small panga, to a wolf who, having calmly walked up to me, flop down, lay its head in my lap, and doze off. From a boa constrictor who liked nothing better than to drape over my shoulders and calmly lie still as I took a long walk, to a young Galapagos sea lion who just wanted to snuggle with me on a beach. The common thread about these encounters was the quiet that existed. To this day, I crave that quiet, as I believe it's when nature is most likely to come calling and is most open to us. In today's world, I lament that there is so little quiet; there is too much clatter, babbling, vocal distraction, intrusive mechanical noise.

The current "climate" of our world today (here, "climate" refers to the attitude of many humans towards nature, who see it as something to exploit, control, or exterminate), I mourn, I grieve, and yes, I think you could say "lament." I mourn that many will never experience such opportunities to better know and love the world due to death or outright extinction, or because they have no understanding of creation (they are decidedly "out of step," as Dr. Mingay concludes) and its importance to our own well-being. All life forms, from an old Douglas fir to the gray whale, along with humans, are struggling due to drastic changes in climate. Direct engagement and interaction with the natural world are elemental to being truly human. It is necessary and, I believe, God's will and desire that we experience the "wild" firsthand, that we care for it and steward it, so that we might come to know our Creator more deeply. That creation is struggling must be acknowledged; we cannot turn a blind eye to it, nor should we cease to speak up about it, even if it draws "negative attention" (Connie Braun states this wonderfully as the "poetry of witness").

Climate of Lament is a reflection of the stress, the sorrow, and the regret that so many of us are feeling. Here, artists, students, and professional academics have bared their souls in their poetry and reflections, willing to lament openly, allowing all of us who read their words to know that we are not alone in our sorrow. I want to join them by briefly relating two stories, one short and one longer, to illustrate what I will/do sorely miss (and what we all stand to lose) due to the current climatic state of our planet. I tell these two stories because they have a direct connection to the event that Dr. Ferber mentions in the introduction. The first took place in an old-growth Douglas fir forest in Whidbey Island State Park. There stood an old, fire-scarred tree with a trunk that a group of twenty-plus college students, with arms stretched wide, could not completely encircle. The ground beneath it was a lush, spongy green cushion, offering shade from the hot sun. I caressed its trunk, breathed in its sweet scent, and heard its whispers as a breeze moved through its crown; it was heavenly and sobering. I wondered what stories that tree could tell about its several-hundred-year life. It had seen so much, and yet, praise God, was (and is) still standing, one that has escaped the chainsaw.

Here is the second story. While visiting San Juan Island, Washington, with a group of students in my marine mammals class at the Au Sable Institute, I had my first up-close encounter with a member of the Southern Resident J-, K-, and L-pod orca community. In the late 1990s and early 2000s, every July, it was almost certain that you could see these orca pods on the west side of San Juan Island, in Haro Strait, doing what came to be affectionately known as the "west-side shuffle." This was indeed one of those days. We had already seen them go north past our vantage point at the Lime Kiln State Park lookout, close to shore, and then go up past the lighthouse, turn around, and then come south past that same lookout about an hour later. Several hours hence, we decided to head back to Lime Kiln to await their return north, for there was every indication that as they spread out, they would all turn around at some point and pass the lookout again. Since no student was eager to leave and catch a ferry back to Whidbey Island, our home base, I suggested we stay and take a later ferry. I left the students at the lookout to wait and watch while I headed north up a winding path to the lighthouse to get further information on what the Southern Residents had been doing that week. As I walked along the path to the lighthouse, with Haro Strait on my left, I found myself at a point where the path dips down rather precariously (and dangerously) close to the water. There was a loud "whoosh" and then I felt a drenching mist as a large male orca, either Blackberry or Mike, surfaced at just that moment. To my further surprise, he maintained his position in the water high enough so that he could give me a visual "once over!" He was so close that had I reached out, I think I would have touched him. As I stumbled further along the path, I became aware that this orca was traveling with me toward the lighthouse, its eye still looking at me! He went a bit further, did something of a fluke flip (perhaps trying for another chance at showering me?) and continued north with me. What the heck!? I think he must have smiled as he pulled away from me, leaving me to wonder what had just happened. Ultimately, he came south again to Lime Kiln, hung out with his family and friends, and then they all headed north, well after sunset. By way of personal lament, I end this story with the reality that the Southern Resident orca pods now rarely engage in that west-side shuffle; they need food, and in that area, there is little to be found. They now spend more time further north and further from shore. I miss that magical summer event. Now, ask yourself—what is the connection between an old Douglas fir and those Southern Resident orcas?

I have taught alongside Dr. Ferber multiple times at the Au Sable Institute, and I well remember the situation Dr. Ferber describes in the introduction. We were on an integrative trip to the Olympic Mountains–talking about the connections between forest, alpine, and marine systems. I can see us on Hurricane Ridge, at that overlook, on a smoky August day in 2018. I was emotionally drained from personal, work, and research-related issues, along with navigating the chaos of two fires and a devastating mud-debris slide back in Santa Barbara, California. I wasn't sure that I could handle the rigor of the five-week session that summer. However, despite the course's intensity, it was also quite uplifting, even though I was at the very end of my emotional tether.

My contribution to the discussion on that August day was to show the connection between 1) the loss of watershed in the forests, due not only to fire but also to indiscriminate logging operations, insect invasion, etc., and 2) the health and strength of glacial melt, especially stream and river flow through the forests, down the mountains, out to the river deltas, and eventually to the ocean. The "connection" lesson (linking the alpine and forest ecology courses with the marine courses) was that, without the free and clean flow of water filtered through the watershed of the forests, there could be no abundant, healthy salmon for resident orca and other marine creatures to feed on. I was doing pretty well until I got to the point where I had to relay the information that salmon runs were nowhere near sufficient to support terrestrial animals, such as bears, all the way down to the ocean and areas of the Salish Sea, where the Southern Resident orca search for Chinook salmon. I indicated that one of the reasons that a Southern Resident orca female, named Tahlequah, had lost her newborn calf was because she lacked food to support her pregnancy; her calf, therefore, likely did not get the necessary nourishment and died. It was at that moment I went a bit "off track," describing the unusual event that was taking place as we talked—that she was continuing to carry her dead calf on her rostrum. As I "know" a fair number of the members of J, K, and L pods on sight, it was as though a good friend was going through the trauma of a miscarriage . . . and . . . I "lost it." As I mentioned earlier, I strive to avoid uncontrollable emotions in public settings, especially when trying to maintain the academic environment necessary for conveying important scientific information; it doesn't seem professional. But I started weeping, and even as I continued to try and "pull it together" to finish what I had to say, I could not speak, as the tears were streaming down my face. It only became even more difficult as Au Sable faculty, staff, and students, also began to weep. I have no idea what other public visitors to the park thought (and there were many listening in on our discussion or passing within earshot), but a collective weeping—yes, a collective lament—was taking place.

These reminiscences are memories of tearful joy, moments of worship, and heart-deep gratefulness for God's creative work on this beautiful planet. But, as I think more about those pleasant memories, as well as losses experienced in my lifetime (which this collection of poems caused me to relive in my mind), I must also acknowledge that my active seeking of connection allowed for these experiences. Many of us have lost our connection to, even our interest in, the living world.

And so, I come to the purpose of this collection of laments, Dr. Ferber and Dr. Mingay's shared "attempt to find a resting place for a multitude of voices and sources of grief and despair about our climatic world in language that is at once academic, personal, and creative."[1] As Drs. Ferber and Mingay came to recognize their academic common ground, they also concluded that no matter what your discipline or scholarly or professional approach, poetry is a form of art that can touch both soul and heart. As all who have contributed to this volume would likely agree, "poetry [*can be*] not only a bridge between arts and science but also a path toward a more rewarding form of lament."[2] Ah! The reason for this volume.

Just what is it to lament? What is the meaning of lamentation? The *Oxford Dictionary* defines a lament or lamentation as "a passionate expression of grief or sorrow,"[3] and to engage in the action of lamenting is to mourn that which has been lost or has died. Biblically, it is the expression of sorrow, grief, or regret over a loss and, notably, may occur in a public or formal way. For me, it means a way to pray to God and turn to him, to give up to him my pain, my suffering, as I seek from him guidance and comfort. If you take a moment to ponder the title *Climate of Lament*, you see an intriguing "play" on words, as the contributors grieve and regret the loss of biodiversity, the destruction of habitat and ecosystem, the fouling of water and soil, the complete upending of climatic conditions on this amazing planet, and most all of the loss and destruction as a result of human-induced global climate change. We

1. p. xxvi.
2. p. xxxii.
3. *Oxford English Dictionary*, "Lamentation."

are living in a degraded and altered climate, which has prompted contributors to this volume to lament openly the loss it has caused.

And why would it be, why should it be, important for us, especially people of faith, to practice lament? (Notice that the word "practice" implies an action will be necessary.) Certainly, to *show us how to demonstrate our grief, fully and truly, to acknowledge that which are indeed real losses in our life on this planet, and to relinquish that which we treasure and deem as lost fully* (I have made something of an alteration here, based on the words of Drs. Ferber and Mingay). For myself, those losses come in many forms—the unearthly silence that now persists in forests where wolves used to roam. Or the organismal silence within the oceans that now is more common, as baleen whales grow silent in their calls, especially in warmer waters, too busy and focused on trying to find the food, never mind finding a mate and reproducing (of course our ships, oil drilling, military activities, etc., make it even harder for the whales to hear each other, even if they were calling to one another). There is the loss of orca I could call and recognize by name: Everett, a young male Southern Resident who seemed to be every orca calf's big brother; Ruffles, the iconic Southern Resident male with that overly tall, wavy dorsal fin, gone now, too. There is Ocean Sun, the last, oldest matriarch of L pod, who is likely the only Southern Resident orca living today who can remember the terrible, cruel round-up of young orca for the aquarium trade that took place in Penn Cove, Washington, in the 1970s that Natalie Crockett's contribution refers to. At last count in early July 2025, Ocean Sun is still with us, but she is getting on in years. I don't want to mourn and grieve the loss of her, but I know it will come; it will be a time to lament, indeed. I continue to be faced with depressingly bare rock in many tide pool areas, nary a sea star in sight, gone due to a bacterial epidemic. We now also see imbalance—on other rocks, too many mussels crowd out other species, as there are no sea stars to keep the mussels in check. But even as I lament, acknowledging an end to that which I have experienced with joy and awe, laughter and "happy tears," lament may now perhaps be seen as a beginning. It allows me the freedom to clearly notice, to speak the truth, even as it hurts, and to nourish and support both human and more than human voices that are speaking to us, telling us their stories of pain, and the possibility, the hope, that they have the capacity to show resilience and renewal. This volume, these poems, I believe, are intended to uphold and encourage that new beginning, through a renewal and return to the practice of lament.

As I read through the poems and reflections, each touched me in some way. I discovered so many ideas, thoughts, and emotions that I had begun to incorporate into this foreword even before I had read all of the entries! I sympathized with those that dealt with loss through fire, or loss of people and culture through gross acts of neglect, fear, and even disrespect. I most certainly and deeply resonated with Natalie Crockett's questions regarding Tokitae, as well as Peter Mahaffy's contemplation of coral reef building and its demise as a result of ocean acidification. Indeed, all of the contributions gave to me in some deeply meaningful way. I took comfort in the fact that I am not alone in my grief, my sorrow, my loss. Lament, as displayed in these chapters, was a welcome form of catharsis, of release. I trust that you will allow yourself that comfort—of being in community with "others" as you read the entries.

Each of the poems is a unique and honest form of lament and prayer. I would ask you to take them to heart—please, allow them to empower you to commit to lament yourself. *You* are indeed not alone in your grief. Take your pain and turn it into hope by working in God's created world: plant a garden, paint a scene of a lush green forest, or jump for joy when you see a salmon leap through the water. As contributor Liana DePoe-Rix states, "while it's true we need our grief, it isn't an option to admit defeat."[4] May these poems encourage you to persevere and work well in his created world.

God's blessings upon you,
Elizabeth (Beth) Horvath
Santa Barbara, CA

4. p. [X-REF]

Foreword

You have in your hands a book that invites you into a global community that is squarely and honestly facing the facts of a planet in dire climate crisis. It is decidedly not a book meant to inspire the sort of unjustified hope with which many people placate and excuse themselves. This book, rather, is for all of us who know enough—and care enough—to grieve for the suffering of creation. What the contributors offer to those of us who are broken by our very love for the world is a way to process and give form to our grief. By their example, they show us the power of poetic lament— an expressive form that is available to all, whether we consider ourselves poets or not. Such poetry, these authors show, can move us out of numbing despair toward inspired agency. Thus, poetry itself becomes a means of resistance against ecological exploitation and environmental injustice. The poems and reflections in this book reveal new insights into our very selves and yield new understanding of the narratives that drive us. At the same time, the poetry of lament makes possible the collective sharing of our deep grief with others of like heart and mind.

When I was a university student, my mother, at the age of forty-two, died suddenly of what the medical examiner termed an accidental overdose of alcohol and prescription medication. What all her children also knew to be true, though, was that her death was the culmination of years of abuse at the hands of my father. After the funeral, I retreated to the place where I always went when I most needed the presence of God: the wilderness around Lake

Cavanaugh, in the foothills of the Cascade mountains. As I walked through the forest, I wept aloud, venting my grief. When I reached the top of a hill where the trail began to descend, I was shocked to see that the entire valley below had been clear cut. In my despair, I continued through the wasteland of stumps and charred burn piles to find the river below—already choked with debris and silt from the eroding hillsides.

Devastated, the only response that seemed right was to give shape to a song of lament—to compose a poem that would give voice to my own grief as well as what I imagined to be the grief of the local community. In one stanza of that poem, I wrote,

> The wind whispered the sad news among the firs
> And the river cast her tears upon the shore
> For rebel man was coming, to torture his brothers the trees
> And afflict sister river with his foul disease.

Ironically, in that moment I really thought that my verses were only about the careless exploitation of the valley's ecosystem. It wasn't until later, when I shared it with others, that I came to understand that my poem was at the same time a lament for my mother's life. The act of writing a lament connected me to the deep anger I felt—about the abuse of the valley, but also, it turned out, about the abuse of my mother. When I shared my poem with those close to me, invariably, the song brought our common feelings into the open and created a cathartic space where we shared our loss as a community. Importantly, I came to understand that my community of lament also included the more-than-human beings in the family of creation, who helped shape my words and lent form to my feelings. As Indigenous theologian Randy Woodley put it when I told him this story, nature mourned with me; nature mourned for me. The act of composing poetry in concert with creation thus helped me to discover my heart's cry and showed me to myself.

I should note that this was the first poem I had ever created—but certainly not the last. Once I had experienced the power of poetry, it continued to be an important mode of expression in my life—particularly in difficult times. That, it seems to me, has much to do with a major purpose in *Climate of Lament*: to urge us to embrace and practice poetry as a means of lament, both individually and collectively. To do so, we need not be poets in the formal sense of the word. Some of the poems in this volume might not meet the standards of artistic excellence according to literary conventions. But that is neither the goal nor the point. Instead, these poetic offerings model for us a means of expression that allows us to voice our deepest sentiments—to ourselves and to one another—in language of the heart. The writers in this book, by courageous example, resist the exclusive standards of that rarefied domain where (we often assume) "real" poetry resides. Indeed, in their vulnerability to share these poems, they help democratize poetry as a common language of soul-expression—accessible to all of us.

A core premise implied through *Climate of Lament* is this: if we have enough courage and integrity to see the suffering state of our planet through an honest lens, then we cannot help but mourn. Yet, we would be wise not to do so in isolation, where it is too easy to slip into despondency and despair. Rather, it is better to mourn with others of like heart and mind. This book, when understood as a "conversation" of sorts, is a reflection of that principle, even as it shows us how to practice it. The poetry of lament gives us permission to grieve; it offers us aesthetic language to express our heart's cry. It especially gives us a means to connect with the wider community of creation—both human and more than human—that can hear and hold our grief, and keep us focused on authentic hope.

Because the poetry of lament is in great part about exposing and proclaiming sometimes hard truths, it offers an alternative to false hope. The writers in this volume look past the comforting narratives that reassure us that everything will turn out OK in the end—or that there is nothing wrong in the first place. And they show us that a more honest hope must be a hope held in light of and despite hard realities—and that honest hope is much harder to find and even harder to sustain.

In my podcast, I always ask my guests one question toward the end of our conversations: "Are you hopeful about our climate future?" Some claim that human behavior is changing fast enough to prevent the worst of our climate crisis. Others put their hope in technology's capacities to save us from ourselves. The more compelling responses, though, come from those who believe that in light of our current climate trajectory, there is no reasonable hope that human action might save us. According to these folks, they define "hope" as commitment to action: to doing the right thing and actively loving creation, even though they know they won't change the world. Others take active hope a step further and hold fast to their conviction that there is a God who loves this world enough to somehow save it from annihilation. The Christ they follow is the Lord of Creation, whose promises of salvation, healing, and restoration extend to the whole of creation, both human and more than human.

It is in light of such honest hope that the poetry of lament—as modeled for us in Scripture, and modeled for us in this very book—is a right and fitting response to the climate crisis. For it is lament that proclaims what right action looks like, and it is lament that gives us the language of prayer by which we can cry mercy to the Creator who loves us all.

Forrest Inslee
Camano Island, WA

Acknowledgments

We are deeply grateful to the contributors of *Climate of Lament*, who responded to our unusual invitation—not for academic papers but for poetic expressions of grief, personal laments rooted in ecological loss and social injustice. Each contributor brought thoughtful and honest engagement to their poems and reflections, shaping a volume that does not turn away from grief, but instead sees it as a path toward awareness and communal responsibility. We thank them not only for their words but for their vulnerability.

We are especially grateful to Beth Horvath and Forrest Inslee for their thoughtful forewords. Beth weeping over Tahlequah inspired the project, and Forrest's enthusiasm encouraged us to see it through to its end. Both scholars made plain the need for a space where academic knowledge and ecological pain could coexist.

We are also indebted to our families for their patience and encouragement throughout the production of this project. We also acknowledge our dogs, Scout and Poppy, who ensured that long, contemplative walks would be part of the book's progress.

Finally, we are grateful to The King's University for its support of projects such as *Climate of Lament*, and for the community it creates for instructors and students. Philip is especially thankful for the sabbatical opportunity to bring the book to completion. Michael is grateful for the partnership between The King's University and the Au Sable Institute of Environmental Studies, which provided fertile ground for this project to grow.

Introduction

As friends and colleagues at The King's University in Edmonton, Alberta, we work in two seemingly disparate fields—Philip Mingay in English literature and Michael Ferber previously in human geography. Philip specializes in portraits of artists in postcolonial literature, and Michael began in the geography of religion and environmental studies, and is now dean of business with a focus on sustainable business. During the COVID-19 pandemic, our regular walks in Edmonton's River Valley became a kind of informal seminar, spaces where personal concerns met the demands of scholarship. Although we came from different fields, we found ourselves drawn to a common desire to discuss the climate crisis in ways that felt emotionally resonant, not just intellectually rigorous. Academic writing, we realized, often lacks room for the grief, vulnerability, and urgency this crisis provokes. As Barry Golding and Annette Foley write in *Constructing Narratives in Later Life*, the use of the personal "I" signals that "the story we choose to write about changes according to the context in which it is retold."[1] Tami Spry similarly suggests that human experience is "chaotic and messy," and thus demands interpretive methods capable of holding that complexity.[2] Even Elizabeth Kolbert, in *Climate Change from A to Z*, admits that "climate change resists narrative—and yet some account of what is happening is needed."[3]

1. Golding and Foley, "Constructing Narratives in Later Life," 387.
2. Spry, "Performing Autoethnography," 727.
3. Kolbert, "Climate Change from A to Z," first header.

In *Climate of Lament*, we attempt to find a resting place for a multitude of voices and sources of grief and despair about our climatic world in language that is at once academic, personal, and creative. These voices are from across the academy and beyond, organized alphabetically by first name rather than professional title, to reflect a central aim of this project: to flatten hierarchies and elevate lament as a shared human response to environmental grief. Contributors include university faculty, theologians, poets, scientists, and undergraduate students, each of whom was invited to write both a poetic lament and a brief prose reflection. These two forms sit in dialogue throughout the book, one giving emotional shape to grief, the other offering personal, philosophical, or contextual insight. What results is a mosaic of perspectives: academic and affective, lyrical and analytical, urgent and meditative. Combined, they embody the conviction that lament is not a retreat from reality but a mode of bearing witness that can catalyze transformation.

We are not alone in turning to poetry in troubled times; other works have similarly sought solace and insight through verse. Our volume is not unlike collections such as Bate and Byrne's *Stressed, Unstressed: Classic Poems to Ease the Mind*, in which they posit that reading poetry has a direct, positive physiological effect on the human body.[4] Other books that contain similar themes are *Love Your Mother: 50 States, 50 Stories, and 50 Women United for Climate Justice*[5] and *Footprints: An Anthology of New Ecopoetry.*[6] Although these books, like ours, recognize the power of art for both resistance and hope and call upon poets and authors from a variety of regions and occupations to show that "new ways of living and thinking . . . are possible,"[7] they are not rooted in the process of lament. Instead, we envision writing one's own lament as a way to counter the ideologies that fuel the climate crisis.

---

4. Bate and Byrne, *Stressed, Unstressed*, 16.

5. McDuff, *Love Your Mother*.

6. Kent and Baylis, *Footprints*.

7. Kent and Baylis, *Footprints*, dust jacket.

While grief and lament are often intertwined, we see it as essential to distinguish between them. Grief is an emotional response to loss, but lament is something more: it is an intentional, often public act of grief that demands recognition or response. Soong-Chan Rah argues that lament is a form of protest, a theological and ethical articulation of suffering in a world that prefers triumphalism or denial.[8] Walter Brueggemann similarly sees lament as a prophetic response that disrupts false ideologies and opens the possibility for renewal.[9] In *Climate of Lament*, the poetry and reflections you will read are not only expressions of grief but acts of lament, naming environmental loss, exposing its ideological roots, and bearing witness in the hope of transformation.

Further, these laments represent a wide range (geographically, academically, and creatively) of poetic and prose responses to environmental degradation. Connie Braun's entry is adamant that lament is a cry "against despair," and inherent in her poems is the "historical ground, the foundation, the deep paternalistic and patriarchal systems of institutions—educational, legal, economic, health, and religious—that govern Western thought and society and privilege the few,"[10] inevitably leading to environmental disaster. Poet Alice Major provides the reader with mediations on silence and the necessity of quiet to understand the "paradox of our human cacophony—it is sound that keeps us from hearing." Ironically, says Major, the COVID-19 pandemic returned silence to our world, and "in the breathing space / offered up by silence, suddenly / we could hear the birds."[11] To bridge the climate of lament in the past and present, Jane Satterfield returns to the Victorian poet, novelist, and environmentalist Emily Brontë in "Emily Brontë's Advice for the Anthropocene." By reenvisioning Brontë, Satterfield writes "against an awareness of human encroachment and the deleterious effects of climate crisis, with the hopes that

8. Rah, *Prophetic Lament*, 21.

9. Brueggemann, *Reality, Grief, Hope*, 25.

10. p. 27.

11. p. 2.

documentation of grief may offer healing, and, possibly inspire action born of love for a more-than-human world."[12]

Our volume also includes a variety of voices of lament, including university undergraduates. For example, Edudzinam Aklamanu's poem, "Foreseen Death," and its accompanying reflection offer a vivid portrayal of ecological grief through the lens of the 2016 Fort McMurray, Alberta, fire. The poem captures the sensory and emotional turmoil residents experienced during the crisis, using evocative imagery to convey the devastation and impending doom that accompanied this natural disaster. Edu's work resonates deeply with the themes of our volume, highlighting the interconnectedness of human actions and environmental consequences. Likewise, Liana DePoe-Rix's poem and reflection delve into the profound sense of ecological grief and the feeling of helplessness that often accompanies it. Written at Pyramid Lake in Jasper, Alberta, the poem captures the delicate interplay between the natural world and the personal experience of mourning in the context of mental health challenges. The poem's transparent, introspective tone and the acknowledgment of one's smallness within the grandeur of nature reflect the themes throughout our volume.

Student submissions are to highlight the power of younger, emotionally immediate voices to engage with ecological lament. These personal and affective perspectives enrich *Climate of Lament* by complementing its more academic reflections about ecological loss. In foregrounding these voices, we aim to present ecological lament not simply as an academic exercise but as a vital and accessible practice, one that belongs to students, emerging scholars, and communities of learning alike.

These personal laments echo a broader pattern of environmental grief now being felt on a global scale, as demonstrated by recent fires that have destroyed areas in Jasper, Alberta, in 2024 and much of Los Angeles, California, in early 2025. However, the origins of this volume go back a few more years. In August of 2018, Michael stood on top of Hurricane Ridge on Washington's Olympic Peninsula with a group of faculty and students from the Au Sable Institute,

12. p. 53.

a national environmental science education program. He was teaching a course on international development and environmental sustainability alongside colleagues instructing Alpine Ecology, Marine Biology, Marine Mammals, Forest Ecology, and Ecological Agriculture. Before arriving at Hurricane Ridge, they spent the previous weeks exploring other local ecosystems to understand the connections between marine and alpine environments in light of human development and climate change. The air was thick with smoke from fires in British Columbia, Washington, and California. In previous years, they could gaze across the Juan de Fuca to Victoria, but this year, visibility was limited to a few miles.

Dr. Beth Horvath, professor of the Au Sable Marine Mammals course, addressed the classes about the situation: her home campus at Westmont College in Santa Barbara had experienced a mandatory evacuation just a few months earlier due to the Thomas Fire and had made national headlines a decade earlier in the infamous Tea Fire.[13] Though fire was top of mind, it was not what elicited a spontaneous group lament on the mountain that morning. Rather, Dr. Horvath's class had been closely following the journey of Tahlequah, the Southern Resident orca (J35), who carried on her rostrum her dead newborn calf for seventeen days. Tahlequah is one of the few remaining Southern Resident orcas still of childbearing age. Southern Resident killer whales are a distinct, endangered population of fish-eating orcas that live in three pods (J, K, L) primarily in the Salish Sea. Their survival is closely tied to Chinook salmon abundance.[14] If the Southern Residents cannot reproduce, they will be functionally extinct in a few years. As Dr. Horvath shared the tragedy of the orca and her calf, she began to weep, and soon, most of the students and faculty joined her in spontaneous lament. There they were, a group of rational scholars and students on the top of a mountain at a public lookout, collectively crying about the state of our natural world, painfully aware that the orca pods are unhealthy because there is no longer enough salmon to sustain their diets.

13. California Department of Forestry and Fire Protection, "Tea Fire."
14. See NOAA Fisheries, "Southern Resident Killer Whale."

Three years later, on June 30, 2021, Michael was planning to drive from his home in Edmonton, Alberta, through British Columbia to return to teach the Au Sable course. Word came that most of the routes were closing due to fire as a massive heat dome parked over the entire Pacific Northwest. As he reviewed routes from Edmonton to Washington State, he was undergoing the second-highest recorded temperature in Edmonton's history. Michael considered driving through Lytton, British Columbia, to experience the country's highest recorded temperature. The day before, Lytton hit a record 49.6° C (121.3° F), hotter than the all-time highs for anywhere in Europe or South America. Many people were flocking there from Vancouver to participate in this climate history, and it was not far off his route. But that afternoon, while considering routes, the excitement in Lytton turned into tragedy as a train sparked a wildfire, and the entire village burned to the ground within hours. Much of British Columbia was charred that summer. Later in the fall, torrential rains fell upon the scorched landscape, creating apocalyptic floods that devastated the region and destroyed every road connecting the lower mainland of British Columbia with the rest of the country.

Then, in the summer of 2024, while in Washington State teaching the same course for Au Sable, Jasper burned. Since 2011, Michael has taken Physical Geography students to multiple sites around Jasper to explore topics such as mountain building, karst systems, erosion, glaciation, and a variety of other themes. Pyramid Lake, the site where Liana DePoe-Rix wrote her poem a year earlier, was spared. But most of the other regular field trip sites were changed for a generation, including Maligne Canyon, Athabasca Falls, and the Jasper townsite itself. Even the church where students would sleep on the floor, the St. Mary and St. George Anglican Parish, was utterly lost. Most of the poems and reflections in this volume were already complete, and yet the scale of lament continues to grow. Together, these three summers trace an arc of intensifying grief. What began as smoke in the distance has now become flame at our doorstep.

The cumulative experiences led to discussions between Philip and Michael, and the possibility emerged of combining science, lament, and poetry in a book for those who have undergone similar grief. As scholars, we are both trained to understand the connections between human activities and natural processes objectively, regardless of discipline. Yet, academics are not taught, and often are ill-equipped, to grapple with the geographies of grief now permeating our world. Amid social tragedies such as the global COVID-19 pandemic, the Russian invasion of Ukraine, student mental health crises, and the proof of mass child graves outside of Canadian Indigenous residential schools, we are also witnessing biodiversity loss on the scale of the sixth mass global extinction and rapidly emerging climate change. These natural and social tragedies inspire laments of anguish in cultures worldwide. Sometimes it is difficult to pinpoint exactly what we are lamenting, given the extensive list of tragedies and disasters. We are working through pain, sorrow, and suffering manifested in the environment due to anthropogenic processes and ideologies of imperialism, colonialism, corporate capitalism, denial, and many others. The scale of global suffering and the extent to which it is realized in local contexts is becoming unfathomable. If we feel this way as professional scholars and educators, how can our students find resiliency?

To name these emotions, scholars and mental health professionals have developed a vocabulary that tries to keep pace with a changing planet, including descriptors such as "solastalgia," "tierra trauma," "climate grief," and "environmental melancholia,"[15] to name a few. However, lament tends to be foreign to our Western culture and is usually only expressed in the context of losing human life. Even contemporary religious congregations have lost what Christopher Wright describes as the willingness, vocabulary, and capacity to engage in authentic lament.[16] In *Prophetic Lament*, Soong-Chan Rah defines this inability to lament as a culture of celebration among globally elite communities who seek constancy and stability of the

---

15. Malcolm, *Words for a Dying World*.
16. Wright, *Message of Lamentations*, 13.

current social order rather than deliverance.[17] Thus, the language of celebration and praise dominates religious liturgy.

In Philip and Michael's discussions, it became clear that despite our differences in scholarly approaches and topics, we had a lot in common, and that poetry was not only a bridge between arts and science but also a path toward a more rewarding form of lament. It is not surprising that the production of poetry rises during significant crises, often composed by people who otherwise do not read the literary form or struggle in their English classes to "understand" poetry. For example, in the aftermath of 9/11 in the United States, more than twenty-five thousand poems were published on poetry.com.[18] Numerous studies have demonstrated that

> poetry allows us to bear witness to who we are and to put into words what often cannot be expressed easily otherwise. Poetry creates avenues for self-expression that cannot be felt through other means of communication. This in itself can be a healing and restorative process, a self-guided therapy that allows us to strengthen our mental health and connection to ourselves, and to those around us.[19]

Scholars and artists alike offer varied accounts of why grief so often finds its way into verse and other creative forms. There are numerous explanations for the relationship between grief and art, including the possibility that poetry supplies a direct catharsis for emotional pain that cannot be solved at that moment through any practical means, even verbally. Instead, there is a yearning for ways to express complicated emotions such as despair and anger, and poetic language, despite its opaqueness, is therapeutic. Further, a poem can be shared instantly through online platforms and groups, connecting poets with other poets who share similar hurt. Communally, poetry, whether it is "good" or "bad," gives purpose, and there is hopeful delight in returning to metaphors, similes,

17. Rah, *Prophetic Lament*, 5.
18. Metres, "Beyond Grief and Grievance.
19. Xiang and Yi, "Look Back," 606.

xx

and other rhetorical devices that we have forgotten but reveal the richness of our world.

For centuries, and certainly since the Romantic period, it has been argued that poetry is no longer relevant—that investments in science and technology are the way out of the mess in which we have found ourselves. However, as the increase in published poetry during times of crisis indicates, artistic expression remains vital. Poetry disrupts the tidy logic of what Walter Brueggemann calls "managed prose," the official language of systems, ideologies, and institutions that seek to keep things as they are.[20] Percy Shelley, writing during the time of nineteenth-century social upheaval, claimed that poetry helps us feel what we otherwise only know.[21] It tears away the veil of familiarity, reminding us of the wonder, and sometimes the horror, of being alive. In times of crisis, poetry doesn't just describe grief. It protests. It refuses silence. It creates a space where emotional truth can confront intellectual denial. Psychologist Margaret Stroebe has noted that poetic language often conveys grief more vividly than scientific language, and that such poetic insights can even generate new understandings for fields like psychology and medicine.[22] It is no surprise that, historically, numerous important scientists were also artists, from Leonardo da Vinci to John James Audubon to Louis Pasteur. In this sense, poetry is not a retreat from rational thought but an urgent companion to it. When we lament poetically, we are not abandoning the world of facts; we are allowing those facts to speak with the weight they deserve. When Michael and his colleagues and students stood on Hurricane Ridge, it was not to formulate a scientific response but to witness and understand the connections among terrestrial, marine, and atmospheric systems from an interdisciplinary perspective, and to do this together in a shared presence. That experience itself was an artistic expression, even a kind of poetry.

While the poetic imagination opens up emotional truth, theological tradition also offers an effective model for confronting

20. Brueggemann, *Reality, Grief, Hope*, 25.

21. Shelley, "Defence of Poetry."

22. Stroebe, "Poetry of Grief," 69.

despair. In Brueggemann's frame, lament is practical because it exposes the ideologies behind suffering and opens space for transformation. In this way, poetry, too, becomes a force that helps us cope, making visible the consequences of harmful ideologies by giving them form and voice. While much contemporary scholarship rightly uncovers the roots of ecological and social decline, it can also leave readers in a state of paralysis, eliciting anxiety and depression without a path forward. Poems of lament, by contrast, enter these emotional landscapes, not to escape them but to name what is broken. In doing so, they help expose the very ideologies that sustain destruction. Lament is not ideologically neutral, and it disrupts false assurances and forces us to confront the uncomfortable environmental reality that is now unfolding before us. Poetry, then, does not merely describe grief. It gives it shape, and in that shaping, opens the door to hope.

The representation of the natural world in literature, and poetry in particular, is a complicated one. Ecocritics have long argued that nature is resistant to linguistic interpretation, despite our intentions or religious instructions to have "dominion over the fish of the sea and over the birds of the air and over every living thing that moves on the earth."[23] In *Climate of Lament*, we believe that poetry is a form of altered language that offers opportunities to lament. Of course, people have always written poetry to "defamiliarize," to "create the sensation of seeing, and not merely recognizing, things," as Russian formalist Viktor Shklovsky pointed out in 1917 in his essay "Art as Device."[24] It unnerves the normal enough for us to see differently, or perhaps more clearly, what was right in front of us. It helps us get our house in order beyond the limitations of our professional language.

In *Reality, Grief, Hope: Three Urgent Prophetic Tasks*, Walter Brueggemann opens up the Book of Lamentations to demonstrate how theological denial, not unlike contemporary climate denial, prevented leaders in ancient Jerusalem from accepting the reality that Babylon could defeat the city. In the case of Jerusalem, the

23. Gen 1:26.
24. Shklovsky, "Art, as Device," 162.

ideology was rooted in the belief that God had blessed Jerusalem and would never allow anything disastrous to happen to it. This ideology held until reality brought it crashing down with unimaginable suffering. An eighteen-month siege cutting off food supplies led to the savagery of strategically planned starvation, disease, and death. The charred remains of the final battle can still be seen in archeological digs. Christopher Wright captures the ideological fall in his commentary on Lamentations:

> Not only was there massive human suffering at every level of physical and emotional experience, not only the devastating demolition and incineration of their ancient and beautiful city, there was also the utter humiliation of their national pride . . . All gone. What possible future could there be? And how could the present even be endured? It is out of that unspeakable pain that Lamentations speaks, daring to describe the indescribable and to utter the unutterable gash and to do so in poetry of astonishing beauty and intricacy, though soaked in tears.[25]

Brueggemann recognizes the power of poetry to capture the prophetic task in times when horrifying reality crushes false ideologies. To critique and unmask an ideology that captivates is to draw attention to the reality of lived experience, which consistently resists being shaped by the ideology's claims.[26] The Old Testament prophets were voices of unrelenting realism juxtaposed against ideological deception. Such courage and freedom to speak out against powers and principalities sometimes breaks the bubbles of illusion.[27]

These ancient ideologies, rooted in divine exceptionalism and national security, are mirrored in our own time through forms no less dangerous: colonial entitlement, extractive capitalism, climate denial, and technocratic rationalism, to name a few. Throughout this volume, we will return to these forces as central subjects of lament. They shape how social and environmental degradation is

25. Wright, *The Message of Lamentations*, 25.
26. Brueggemann, *Reality, Grief, Hope*, 15.
27. Brueggemann, *Reality, Grief, Hope*, 24.

rationalized, how suffering is distributed, and how change is resisted. The conclusion will name these and other ideologies directly, inviting readers to confront the powers behind the grief and the possibility of reimagined futures beyond them.

The fall of Jerusalem did not happen out of the blue. The prophets uttered warning after warning, and Jeremiah had even written words on a scroll twenty-three years earlier, hoping that things would not unfold as they did. How did King Jehoiakim receive that scroll? He burnt it. Scientists, the prophets of our day, are crying out warnings of impending disaster if we do not change our ways. But we are tied to our ideologies. Our prophetic task, in the words of Brueggemann, "amid a culture of denial, is to embrace, model, and practice grief, in order that the real losses in our lives can be acknowledged. The purpose of such a performance of sadness is so that the things we deeply treasure among us and have lost may be fully relinquished."[28] And thus, we anticipate that a volume of environmental and social laments linked to climate change might help us move toward new ways of being. We hope this book can demonstrate how poems of environmental lament draw observers to pain, sorrow, and suffering, and thus evoke the facts of on-the-ground realism into contemporary orientations of celebratory denial.

28. Brueggemann, *Reality, Grief, Hope*, 79.

1

Alice Major

City Birds Sing Louder

City birds sing louder
. . . than their country counterparts,
pitching their syrinxes in competition
with train track rattle, traffic cacophony,
garbage truck growl and fart,
industry's whack-a-mole—one drill stops,
another engine surges in to cram the gap.
In all the clang-clang-clanging decibels,
smaller warbles sink below the aural
clamor. A magpie needs to up its screech
to conquer the inflationary spiral
of noise. Starlings, apparently, must reach
jackhammer levels to be heard.
Until pandemic's impact—a wave
of lockdown silence settles, antiviral,
in the planet's vibrating crust
and Earth can hear herself,
her underlying shifts and tremors,
clearer when our grinding gears

go calm and quiet.
And with the seismic relaxation
of the city's din, in the breathing space
offered up by silence, suddenly
we can hear the birds.

Reflection

The early weeks and months of the COVID-19 pandemic offered us an unexpected reprieve from the noise that humanity makes. After lockdowns came into force around the world, an international group of seismologists from thirty-three countries measured a drop of up to 50 percent in so-called urban ambient noise that's generated by humans traveling and factories humming.[1] Lower background noise during lockdowns meant measuring stations could pick up small earthquakes that otherwise would not be observed.

Yes, humans make that much noise. We can drown out the rumblings of the planet herself.

My poem was inspired by the finding from various studies that city-dwelling birds have to cope with our clamor by singing measurably higher and louder than their country cousins.[2] During those quieted days of lockdown, people in cities from London to Rome to Burnaby, British Columbia, reported suddenly being able to hear birdsong—even though birds were actually singing less loudly than usual in city environments. In one study,[3] white-throated sparrows in San Francisco were singing one-third softer, on average, than they had before the lockdown—and their songs covered a wider spectrum of sound. They didn't have to shriek so much at higher frequencies in order to be heard.

I sympathize with the birds. In my city of Edmonton, Alberta, which seems to have become so much noisier than it was when I arrived here four decades ago, I frequently crave quiet—a physical

1. Subramanian et al., "Global Quieting," 1338–39.
2. Nemeth, "Clamorous City Blackbirds."
3. Goldman, "Bird Song Became Softer."

hunger to not hear the leaf blowers and lawn mowers, the gray-white noise of constant traffic on the Yellowhead Highway a couple of miles away, or the sirens along 111 Avenue.

Of course, humans have been complaining about the noise we make as long as we've been assembling cities. In the two thousand-year-old epic of Gilgamesh, the great god Enlil was aroused by the clamor of the city of Shuruppak and told the other gods in council, "The uproar of mankind is intolerable and sleep is no longer possible by reason of the babble."[4]

"Babble." The human voice in all its strident frequencies. Crowded restaurants and roaring stadiums. Reverberating, indistinguishable announcements over loudspeaker systems. Diatribe and opinion and insult—frenetic arguments about whether climate change is real or masks take away "freedom." Everything we have to listen to from the seat behind us on the bus. And the tinny buzz from the earphones of the passenger beside us.

Our attention is jerked to heel by language. We are innately disposed to pay attention to it from birth. Our earliest months are spent sorting out which noises are meaningful in the wash of sound waves that other humans around us are making with their large, constantly moving mouths. To the end of our lives, we can't stop automatically trying to listen for words—they pop intrusively from the murmur of a radio program in another room to snag my attention . . . Ukraine . . . COVID . . . convoy. Immediately, my brain tries to make narrative of them, put them into context. The language compulsion is so ingrained that even in an MRI machine, the weird chugging whine starts to sound like words. It may sound strange, coming from a poet, that sometimes I long to get away from human words and the demand that I decipher their meaning, but I do.

However, most of the modern sounds humanity makes—the ones that disturb seismic measuring stations—are not meant to be meaningful. They're simply by-products of industrial processes, mindlessly operating. We can tune it out for the most part, yet we register the auditory clutter unconsciously. And it seems to hound me even in places where I'd hope to get away. On the tranquil paths

4. Dalley, *Myths from Mesopotamia*, 109–11.

of the University of Alberta's Botanic Garden, thirty kilometers from the city, the hum and truck-roar of Highway 60 washes in constantly. Hiking a trail on the bench-lands above the townsite of Jasper, where vistas of the river valley open into a majestic distance—well, there's that buzz again from the TransCanada highway, the sound that is too continuous and human-made to be the variable sift of wind and trees.

Of course, there is no such thing as complete silence. The world is always in motion, stirring up vibrations that find their way to our ears. I'm not asking for utter blackness, noise-canceling headphones, the dearth of any molecular movement. What I am craving is to hear something else besides the cycling of our human noise; I'm like a seismic monitor wanting to hear the planet herself.

When we can hear the nonhuman noises—wind, water, grass, thunder—they give us information we need about the environment around us. But most of all, we listen for the sounds that are not human but are intentional. Especially birdsong. We realize that comes to us from the world of conscious, animal life. It is not the mechanical clank and whine we grow so used to. It occupies a liminal space: it conveys meaning, but it's not meaning that my brain has to translate.

In my city now, the soundscape of birdsong has become so much quieter in recent years. Even in the early pandemic months, the dawn chorus of summer robins that used to carol through the neighborhood a couple of decades ago was reduced to one or two voices. Still, birds are mercifully still here. When the furnace cuts out, when the side fan on the neighbor's house goes quiet and the snowblower stops, quiet opens up like a blessing. Into that space will sometimes come the sol-fa notes of a chickadee or the house sparrow's chirrup. I don't have to understand what they are communicating, but it has meaning for the birds. For me, it simply means peace.

Until, again, that fan starts up.

The paradox of our human cacophony—it is sound that keeps us from hearing; it is sound that claims our attention but prevents us from paying it.

2

Ashley Sakundiak

Lifeless

She was once full of life.
Energized by the wind
Reaching for the clouds
Nourishing those who depended on her existence.
She was loved by many, and never alone
But when appreciation dissipated, so did her passion for life.
She is parched from others, taking more than giving
Her body once full of life
Now nourishes no one.
She is lifeless, apathetic, and wilted over.
The conditions are to blame, for the loss of such a vibrant soul.

Reflection

Envision a mosaic of brown painted over a familiar prairie landscape. Combine this view with dehydration, looming death, and an overwhelming sense of devastation. This describes the drought of 2021 that my family, and many others, experienced in rural Alberta. During the COVID-19 pandemic, I was living back home on an acreage north of Vermilion, where I grew up with my three siblings, raising sheep. In a family operation, there is an unspoken obligation and responsibility to contribute to the everyday chores and tasks necessary to raising livestock. Despite not owning any of the flock at this time, I can vividly recall the fear and stress endured over the long, dry summer months. Although this drought was not the only one my family experienced in their fifteen years of raising sheep, it was the most severe. Fortunately, we found pastures to rent, as ours was far from sufficient for grazing. However, the rented pastures had poor fencing, no water supplies, and were not large enough to host the entire flock. These conditions led to considerably more work, including fencing, hauling water from home, dividing up the flock, and frequently rotating the pastures. Despite the extra hours of work and countless prayers for rain, the land struggled to provide for our needs.

"Lifeless" reflects these struggles from the perspective of Mother Nature as a personified blade of grass, highlighting the harsh realities of climate change due to human carelessness. Watching the pasture from my bedroom window, that no longer provides for the flock of sheep that depend on it, is alarming. Seeing the grass become bleached by the sun and the uncertainty around when the fields will be replenished with nutrients amplifies my fear over the well-being of our livestock. Throughout my experience raising sheep, each drought has been more severe than the last, with the 2021 drought being no exception. This trend predicts that future droughts will continue to worsen if people do not change their ways. It is interesting to note that my childhood acreage has a sand base, revealing historical evidence of a prior desert and poorly vegetated land. Despite decades of strong nutrients and bountiful pastures, the recent drought displays cyclical geographical patterns and a transition towards depleting pastures. My grief over witnessing a dying pasture at my childhood home is deeply rooted within my fear of transitioning into new phases of my life. Losing the place that nurtured me and fostered my development feels like losing a piece of my foundational identity. This pasture is more than a fenced plot of land; it is where my siblings and I learned how to raise livestock—a place where relationships developed and a passion for the agriculture industry blossomed. This pasture is meant to nurture new life and create opportunities for development, not abandon its habitants while fighting for its life. The reality is that I do not know what future land conditions may entail, but I do know my love for this pasture, and, therefore, this dying land will not be mourned in vain.

3

Cassidhe Hart

My God!

A Lament

According to Psalm 22. A psalm of Earth.

My God, why have you forsaken me?
Why are you so far from saving me—
so far from my anguished groans?
My God, I cry out to you in the rush of wildfire,
but you don't answer;
even in the heaviest hurricane, I don't stop.

You are the holy one, enthroned.
You are the one for whom every windblown leaf applauds.
Every age, down through the lines of time written in my sediment,
has trusted you to be our saving breath.
Each pulse of life reached out for you and was held.
You sustained all things.

But now I am inanimate, un-souled,
ground down beneath the creatures made of my dust.

All who see me size me up,
shrugging their shoulders:
"God made the Earth,
so let God rescue her.
Let God deliver her,
since God is the one who cares so much."

But you are the one who pulled me
from the womb of being,
speaking me into spinning through space and time.
I was cast on you from my birth;
you've been my God
since I was formed in shadow.
Please don't be far from me,
because trouble is near
and there's no one to help.

Many surround me;
the mighty bulls of commerce encircle me.
They open their mouths at me
like a bulldozer ripping and roaring!
I'm poured out like melted ice caps.
All my forests have fragmented.

My oceans are like wax,
congealed with pockets of petroleum.
My springs are dried up,
soil cracked like pottery.
My skies redden not with dawn
but with smoky haze;
I am set down in the sludge of death.

Satellites surround me,
fleets of airplanes circle me like predators—
my seasons are undone.
I watch my creatures shrivel to bones.

Meanwhile, the powerful just stare at me,
unmoved.
They divvy up my topsoil
among themselves;
they gamble for my precious minerals.

But you, Lord! Don't be far away!
You are my strength!
Come quickly and help me!
Deliver me from the machine of violence.
Save my life from the mouth of greed.

I will declare your name
to everything you have made.
I will praise you to the edges
of the universe!
Because you won't forget
my suffering—
you won't hide your face from me.
No, you will listen when I cry out for help.

Every part of the me
will remember,
every species and element will praise you.
All your dirt-bound creatures
will kiss the ground in reverence.
Our being lives for you.
Future generations will be told
about you.
They will proclaim your justice
to those not yet born,
telling them what the Giver of Life has done.

Reflection

The biblical book of Psalms, a collection of one hundred fifty ancient songs, has supported both Jewish and Christian worship for millennia. Psalm 22 follows the traditional structure of a lament psalm: divine address, complaint, confession of trust, petition, exclamation of certainty, and vow of praise.[1] My reworking of Psalm 22 above imagines the earth herself spilling out these words of anguish before the Creator.

Scientists and lay people alike can find it difficult to engage with the depth and breadth of the climate disaster; climate change is a subject with both vast reach and miniscule scale, swirling with impossible complexity, yet as immanent as drought-dried dirt in the backyard. Images of loss clamor for our attention. An effective response to the climate crisis requires us first to express the grief that both contains and transcends our local experience. Because the psalms move between the grandiose and the deeply personal, their structure can embrace the tensions of global and regional climate distress, giving us a form through which to breathe our laments.

The desperation in this psalm, both originally and rewritten, is raw as the speaker wonders about God's presence, worries about predatory enemies, and describes the wholesale plundering of their well-being. Through these words, we can hear, see, taste, touch, and smell the pain of a crucified planet. Concurrently, the lament touches a cosmic experience of loss and moves through the far-reaching systems of oppression responsible for the violence. The individual acts the original psalm describes, varying on the spectrum from apathy to exploitation, map eerily onto the contemporary ecological

1. Encyclopedia Britannica, "Psalms."

impacts of colonialism, racism, sexism, and capitalism. These death-dealing systems appear on both small and global scales. And, critically, these evils do not come from nowhere. This suffering has perpetrators, beings who act with greed or with indifference. When we read the psalm through the voice of the wounded planet, we are confronted with the duality of humanity's voice within the lament. We are the shriveled and suffering, and we are the circling bulls. We are the diminished and oppressed, and we are the ones who shrug our shoulders. In this way, the lament is also a confession. We weep with a strip-mined forest, even as we participate in a culture of consumption that digs up precious minerals for our electronics. We rage at the growing number of days when the city air is unbreathable, but we also know that the darker a person's skin and the less money in their wallet, the more likely it is that factories stand in their neighborhood.[2] The psalm of lament connects not just the local and the global but also a full range of emotional experience: grief and guilt, desolation and culpability. We mourn the crucified, and we stand among the perpetrators.

In the end, the psalm moves its readers to remembering. After the dissolution of tears and the stigmata of suffering, we are brought together again into hope for a future where all is made whole. We can't jump immediately to this end, however. We must start with the grief we know and listen to the pain of the planet where we stand. The lament psalm gives us the structure, and we fill it with our own particularity. When writing about energy shifts, activist Naomi Klein says, "It's neither big nationally owned monopolies nor large corporate-owned . . . operations that have the best track record . . . it's communities, co-ops, and farmers, working within the context of an ambitious, well-designed national framework."[3] The same can be said for shifts in perspective. It is at the level of the communal, rather than only the global or the individual, where hope for the future resides. It is at this level, through our laments, that we can connect the dots between the suffering we see in our local ecosystems and the larger global climate picture—and, perhaps, walk ever closer to justice.

2. Moe-Lobeda, *Resisting Structural Evil*, 36–37.
3. Klein, *This Changes Everything*, 132.

13

4

Connie Braun

"Wisdom resides in the house of mourning," states the writer of Ecclesiastes (7:4). From the subjectivity of a child of postwar refugee immigrants to Canada, these poems in lyric verse and notebook form—"Grief Is a Protest," "Vigil for the Seven Children Who Died in Migrant Detainment Camps,"[1] and "Kneefall"—probe trauma and childhood, and the climate, ecological and spiritual, of lament. Sorrow and suffering manifested in the environmental crises, migrations, racism, and denial, converge in the "house of mourning"—that is, in poems about war, holocaust, migration, and displacement within the human and natural world, past and present. "Abscission" is a cry for change. Holding inextricable connections and carrying the embedded echoes of other voices, these poems of lament engender the attitude and posture of both grief and hope for the potential of transformation.

---

1. Braun, "Vigil for the Seven Children," 1.

14

Grief Is a Protest

What can describe this emptying moment,
this century's catastrophes?

Border walls, internment camps
for infants and children.

Parents have walked thousands of miles
seeking refuge.

The heat of summer.

The orca carries
her grief on her head for a thousand miles,

Tahlequah swims
her dead calf through the water for seventeen days.

Every Friday for a year
young Greta protests plastic in the ocean, the melting ice.

*

When his students asked him about catastrophe
and despair,

the teacher, a survivor, taught them.
Even if everything is hopeless, we must do what we can.

Sadness is the beginning, not the end.
The span and depth of grief,

a desert, an ocean. The attempt to cross,
our dissent.

Vigil for the Seven Children Who Died in Migrant Detainment Camps

Carlos (16), Juan (16), Darla (10), Felipe (8), Jakelin (7), Wilmer (2), and Mariee (20 months)

First pangs as the child roots for the breast.

Some will struggle all their lives.
Or

until peace comes.
We light candles for the children,

speak each name
of the perished, seven morning stars. Or novas.

My small candle stutters.

Silent reverberations.
That which still clings.

I hold up my small flame.
A choir of mothers, sisters of mercy, sing

for each child. Bright flowers,
buttercups and poppies like the ones that grew

in my grandmother's yard,
embroidered on little girls' dresses.

They flutter. She planted a garden,
one just like she had before the children

were pulled up by their roots.
A woman's pain

transforms into birth. "*We are
our grandmother's prayers*"[2]

the circle of women sings. We cry for these atrocities

and sing.[3]

2. Ysaye M. Barnwell, "We Are," track 14 on Sweet Honey in the Rock, *Sacred Ground*, EarthBeat!, 1995.

3. A version of "Vigil for the Seven Children Who Died in Migrant Detainment Camps" was first published by The Alfred Gustav Press, North Vancouver, BC (2020).

Kneefall 2021

The kneefall opened up the way for new forms of collective remembrance and responsibility.[4]

—Valentin Rauer, from "Symbols in Action: Willy Brandt's kneefall at the Warsaw Memorial"

I just sit and listen.[5]

—The late, former Senator Murray Sinclair and former chair of the Truth and Reconciliation Commission

May 26, 2021:

From British Columbia to Japan and Germany, the image goes viral—without cortège, she is prone on a logging truck driving north on the Nanaimo Parkway,

the giant cedar. She will not disappear
without notice, rings of the vanished

who lived beneath the forest's canopy
in her heartwood.

---

4. Rauer, "Symbols in Action," 258.
5. Flanagan, "Murray Sinclair's Fabrications."

When you cannot cry, you cannot breathe.
The trees take breath and cleanse it.

Announced on May 26:

"Pursuant to section 5.1 of the aeronautics act, the airspace surrounding the Tk̓emlúps te Secwépemc Kamloops Indian Band Residential School

is restricted."[6] . . . *"Preliminary detection*

. . . made by a specialist in ground-penetrating radar."[7]

Shoes with laces and buckles. Ballet slippers. Slip-on sneakers. Flip-flops. Rain boots.

On the steps of public buildings across the country, mourners place a pair for each of the children—

some as young as three years old.

215

pairs of shoes to remember

the disappeared children
at the confluence of the river's two branches, the river named in 1808 by the first white man.

The rocks and clay are the ancestors.
Something very profound has been unearthed.

*

6. Larsen, "Airspace," para. 10.
7. Larsen, "Airspace," para. 8.

1910:

An official stated that those schools were

"graced towards

the final solution

of our Indian Problem."[8]

1922:

A doctor wrote *The Story of a National Crime.*[9]

*

Deprivation, disease, despair—
children died

alone.

*Survivors are losing what little hope they had that the children who
went missing during the residential school era*

could still be alive

somewhere,

suspect, quite frankly, that every school had a burial site.[10]

A circle of cedar branches surrounds the faster's lodge.
Inside, cedar branches cover the floor,

8. Department of Indian Affairs: Superintendent D.C. Scott to BC Indian
Agent-General Major D. McKay. DIA Archives, RG 1-Series, Apr. 12, 1910.

9. Bryce, *Story of a National Crime.*

10. Sinclair, "Statement on Residential School Burial."

cedar smoke carries the people's prayer.

*

Sun's gravity and roots of trees hold the earth together.
The tree connects earth and spirit.

Circumference of the millennium, giant cedar, harbinger
of truth.

An apology is not justice. It is a start.
The people are tired of being angry.

Heartwood and heart, spirit and earth,
felled mother and children,

everything is connected—
cedar, children, kneefall.

Abscission

after "Peaceful Transition."[11]

—Tony Hoagland

Climate change requires technologies of the heart: listening, sensing,
relating, loving, embracing, aligning, cohering, transforming.[12]

—Thomas Hübl, modern mystic

The cells between stem and branch
weaken until the leaf

falls

under its own weight
and wind. Yesterday, a tornado warning.

This is the time of abscission.

*

The poet Hoagland hoped for a peaceful
transition, but he is dead.

There are eight years left.

---

11. Hoagland, "Peaceful Transition," in *Unincorporated Persons*.
12. Hübl, "Anatomy of Inaction," COP26, UN Climate Change Conference.

*

True clouds, or smoke, sunlight
reduced, the trees

turning ochre and scarlet early this year, overflowing
with pigment. Unusually

vibrant, carotenoids after drought, flaming

beauty, a sign of trauma, a river

burst
from the sky to soak the trees. The mountain

slid.

*

*"Promises made for a temperature rise this century of 2.7 degrees
Celsius. Net zero commitments could stave off another half a degree,
but the world is still falling short."*[13]

*

Along the route to my house
yellow birch and mountain alder

copses
among pines,

charred bones,
after a season of smoke and fires,

13. Hübl, "Anatomy of Inaction," COP26, UN Climate Change Conference.

a road, my entire life, traveled,
muddied.

*

*"I am hoping the humans will be calm in their diminishing.
That the forests grow back with patience, not rage."*[14]

*

By the time a tall forest has risen from the charr

I will be gone. But for these years of countdown,

humanity falling under its own weight,

for this abscission, the heart must blaze.

14. Hoagland, "Peaceful Transition."

Reflection

The present crises, social, political, environmental, is the result of a failure to imagine that everything is connected.[15]

Lament arises from loss and injustice, a cry of, and against, despair. The irony of the phrase "climate of lament" is that climate is understood to be literal or atmospheric, as well as the existential atmosphere of our time, as we are confronted with wars, migrations, and a countdown of years remaining to reach zero emissions. As we consider the present day, the words of Jesus long ago recorded in Luke 19:40 are poetically thick with meaning: if we "remain silent, the stones will give voice and cry out." In our silence, the earth and all its creatures are crying out.

Over the period these poems were written, migrants around the world had amassed at borders because of violence perpetrated against the vulnerable, and against the earth. At the same time, the youth, inspired by the activism of Greta Thunberg from Sweden, are demanding that world political leaders and the world's few billionaires and industrialists address climate change and the suffering—human, creaturely, and of the planet—caused by it. In the historical, ancestral experience of this poet, of a postwar, refugee-immigrant family, historical traumas speak directly into the present-day, confronting earlier settler and migration narratives and the truth that European postwar refugees immigrated to a country with a silent history of violence against Indigenous peoples and other groups. These generational and collective traumas

15. Solnit, "Slow Change."

26

of the systemic foundations of colonialism, capitalism, and racism have entered our national consciousness.

Poetry lifts language beyond its limits as chosen words carry also the unsaid, the correspondingly significant truths that open the reader to the realm of intuition and imagination, these other ways of knowing, less valued by Western culture. Inherent within these poems, between the lines, is the historical ground, the foundation, the deep paternalistic and patriarchal systems of institutions—educational, legal, economic, health, and religious—that govern Western thought and society and privilege the few. In particular, Duncan Campbell Scott, a celebrated poet of his time (1862–1947), was committed to Canada's colonial project and to "solving" what he termed "the Indian Problem."[16] With other voices, including contemporary poets, the youth, Indigenous voices of Truth and Reconciliation, the songs of women, and "our grandmother's prayers" embedded within them, the poems juxtapose disparate events, past and present, one inextricable from another, in unfolding, tragic irony. Throughout his enduring lifework, the late Elie Wiesel exhorts us, still, to do what we can.[17] As humanity exploits and neglects the earth and the vulnerable, the earth becomes the voice that cries out. The whole world is in crises at every level, and the earth travails like a mother.

The poetry of lament is a refusal to look away, a refusal to remain silent. It is the poetry of witness. In winter 2018, at an art exhibit addressing warming oceans, I heard philosopher and poet Tim Lilburn give a talk wherein he described climate change as an environmental holocaust. In August 2018, in Pacific Northwest waters where the killer whale population was significantly reduced, a resident orca gave birth. The highly anticipated calf lived only moments, and the mother, J35, also known as Tahlequah, carried her dead calf for seventeen days in what scientists described as extreme grief. This mammal mother's grief mirrored the grief of human mothers, as refugees and migrants, families with children,

---

16. National Archives of Canada, Record Group 10, vol. 6810, file 470–72-3, vol. 7, 55 (L-3) and 63 (N-3).

17. Burger, *Witness*.

were fleeing from poverty and hunger as result of climate change (and from war and violence), in a movement of population not seen since the displacements of World War II. In the summer of 2019, cities across North America, including my home city, Vancouver, held vigils for children who died in migrant detainment camps in protest of such places and the policies that permit them. Also, in 2018, a young Swedish girl Greta Thunberg gained renown as she protested climate change. Inspired to environmental activism, the world's youth, speaking truth to power, made their voices heard at the Paris Climate Conference (2021), demanding that their governments meet carbon emissions targets.

The late peace activist and holocaust survivor Elie Wiesel taught his students that sadness and hope are connected as we speak out in the face of injustice or despair. As a first-generation child born in Canada, of German heritage, the image of Willy Brandt falling to his knees in 1970 at the site of the Warsaw Ghetto in Poland becomes a powerful symbol to me for Canada's own truth and reconciliation process. The wisdom of Indigenous peoples and ancient religious traditions teach that everything is connected, just as tree roots are inextricably webbed beneath us. Thus, conversely, social and environmental degradation are not separate; and as human beings of the earth, we have become displaced, not only physically but morally and spiritually. In notebook form, "Kneefall," the title alluding to an act of contrition, begins with two epigraphs and with two separate events from the same day (May 26, 2021), occurring in my province, British Columbia: the sighting of a logging truck carrying a newly felled old-growth log; and the discovery of the first of thousands of sites at former government residential schools, initially reported as "remains"—later reported (November 2024) as "anomalies" in *The National Post*,[18] on the Canadian Broadcasting Corporation, and in other media. But trauma persists. A genocide took place. Children taken never

---

18. Glavin, "Canada Slowly Acknowledging." The article reports the Tk'emlúps te Secwépemc announcement using the term "anomalies" rather than earlier descriptions of "remains," reflecting a shift in the public and journalistic language framing of the findings.

returned to their families. This image of the giant felled old-growth tree, a mother tree, is a visible representation of our disconnection to earth, to one another other, juxtaposed with, and connected to, atrocity.

When humanity remains silent at social and ecological degradation, the earth itself becomes the voice of lament. After the fires and drought of successive summers, in November 2021, my childhood community experienced one of Canada's largest flooding disasters when a massive atmospheric river fell over southern British Columbia. The poem, "Abscission," written in its wake, bears urgency. Lament is the emergence of language from silence, an act and posture that encompasses not only grief but, by the very act of utterance, is the insistence of *hope*. As such, poems of lament are a form of dissent and activism. Implicit in lament is the imagination for a world more whole. A poem of witness or lament is a small candle among all those keeping vigil throughout the night, together, luminous.

5

Cynthia Wallace

Lament for a Gathered Community

Under skies thick with the
smoke of a thousand groaning
trees, our lungs aching with
shameful soot, we join our voices
with a weeping world. Our cells
have betrayed us to cancers of body
and collective soul. Our sisters and
brothers sob or turn aside in
necessary numbness. Our children
weave among us, worrying at
our faces. Behind us, tomato leaves
curl like empty cups reaching up in
the choking toxic air. Meanwhile,
neighbors find graves unmarked
but not surprising, given all they've
always known and said, although we
have not listened: the abuses and the
deprivations, the colonial collusions
with polluted forms of faith.

This is our inheritance: land stolen and
handed around like so much manna. Beloved
humans stolen and harmed and hidden. A
branch of belief so damaged it bears bitter,
killing fruit.

Who are we meant to be, gathered
around this purple juice, this broken
bread, the very air we breathe wounding
our half-open eyes, the children on
our laps wondering at what we
offer? Who are we meant to be,
sitting here in the ash-heaps of
all we thought we ought to build?

Reflection

This poem began as a lament I wrote for the tiny house church that met in my suburban Saskatoon, Saskatchewan, backyard through the summer of 2021, during the height of the summer wildfires. The sky was hazy, the sunlight an eerie red, and each Sunday, I checked the air quality reports to determine if we could safely meet outdoors. Fires burned in the north of Saskatchewan and across the prairies, in British Columbia, and in California. In fact, Natural Resources Canada reports that in Canada alone, 6,156 wildfires burned that year, covering over four million hectares.[1] Even though no fires burned in our own South Saskatchewan River watershed, every breath we took reminded us that the map boundaries our forebears drew mean little in the face of global ecological destruction: we are all neighbors.

At the same time, news was breaking about a growing number of unmarked graves confirmed at the sites of Indian Residential Schools across the landmass we now call Canada. Using ground-penetrating radar, the Tk̓emlúps te Secwépemc people had found the graves of 215 children on the grounds of a former residential school near Kamloops, British Columbia.[2] And then, in June, 751 more unmarked graves were found at the site of the Marieval Indian Residential School, east of Regina, Saskatchewan, by the Cowessess First Nation.[3] The Marieval School operated from 1898 to 1996, one of more than 130 residential schools across Canada that functioned in a partnership of church and state to forcibly separate

1. Natural Resources Canada, "National Wildland and Fire Situation."
2. Lindeman, "Canada."
3. Cecco, "Canada Discovers 751 Unmarked Graves."

First Nations, Inuit, and Métis children from their families and cultures, forcing assimilation to so-called "Canadian" ways in a purposeful attempt now recognized as cultural genocide.[4] More than 150,000 Indigenous children attended these schools, which were rife with abuse. The last schools closed in the late 1990s, well into my lifetime, but I heard almost nothing of this history until I moved from the United States to Saskatchewan in 2013.

Watching my children play in the choking air, I couldn't help seeing the encroaching threats of climate change as inseparable from the history and present force of colonization and its bedfellow, the resource extraction industry—an industry in which current-day Canada is deeply invested, both at home and abroad. I couldn't help but see the violence we do to the earth as part and parcel of the project that ripped other mothers' babies from their arms. And I couldn't help but feel the deep betrayal of my faith tradition's participation in this project through the Doctrine of Discovery that justified colonial seizure of land occupied by non-Christians and the theology of dominion over the earth that justified its destruction. As Sarah Augustine, a Pueblo (Tewa) descendant, explains in *The Land Is Not Empty*,

> The foundational documents of the Doctrine of Discovery are a series of papal bulls, or legal decrees, created by the Christian church that explain why Europeans alone deserve to own land in what was termed the New World, and why those of European descent are deemed human while those Indigenous to the land, my ancestors included, are not.[5]

These fifteenth-century documents theologically justified the European contest for power, land, and wealth in the so-called New World: they used the language of God to normalize cruelty and murderous greed. Robyn Maynard and Leanne Betasamosake Simpson further explain:

---

4. National Centre for Truth and Reconciliation, "Residential School History."

5. Augustine, *Land Is Not Empty*, 19.

> The massive destruction, gendered and murderous, of
> (Indigenous) human life and land dispossession; the
> commodification, exploitation, and fungibility of (Black)
> human life; and the relentless expropriation and de-
> struction of non-human nature are inextricably linked:
> a disregard for all living things except for their value as
> property to be accumulated.[6]

The smoke that burned our eyes and lungs the summer of 2021—
the smoke that has characterized each summer since—refuses to
let us forget this outrage.

What can it mean to have faith at all, given all the harms my
tradition has perpetrated in the name of God? My lament must
layer grief upon grief: grief for the very good creation that groans
in climate crisis; grief for the colonial violence in which I, as a
white settler, am still embedded; and grief at the role the church
has played in these past and present injustices. For me, lamenting
these wrongs is an essential expression of faith in a God whom we
ask, how long? Why do the wicked prosper? I have come to believe
that God holds back from rescuing us—even from ourselves and
from each other—out of respect for our freedom, which is a kind
of love. I don't know how else to square the devastations we are allowed to wreak with the idea of a Christ within whom we live and
move and have our being. In voicing our anguish, we also confess
our collusions. We grow our holy longing for something better.
We admit the limits of our power and the depth of our despair.
Naming this sorrow is the only way I know how to live with integrity, with the smoke stinging my eyes and my neighbors mourning
babies in unmarked graves, babies on reserves without clean water,
babies whose futures are hard to imagine as permafrost melts, and
the bush goes up in flames.

Voicing lament together doesn't solve or resolve anything,
but it fills me with another sensation alongside my despair: not
optimism, or even hope, but accompaniment. I see that my grief
is not mine alone and begin to wonder if, in the space of collective

6. Maynard and Simpson, *Rehearsals for Living*, 23–24 (parentheses and
emphasis in original).

anguish, something new and good might break through. I want all our children to know that we want this for them—something better. But first we must begin by telling the truth.

6

David Rutherford

A Place Transformed

A beautiful coastal floodplain
Dense fog in the early morning
Shore birds twitter in the marsh.
Farm laborers quietly work
In vast agricultural fields.
But development creeps in.
Fields are covered up.
Boulevards radiate throughout.
Long streets lined with block walls
Hide the tract houses ensconced within.
The places I know disappear.
Cars, traffic, signal lights abound.
Suburbia spreads.
Strip malls proliferate.
Where is the quiet?
Nineteen seventy-nine
Main Street and PCH
Huntington Beach, California
Jack's Surfboard Shop, an icon

Displaying identity.
The place is a delight of
"Intimate, undisciplined differentiation."[1]
A unique place
But unique places
Hold little value
In the globalizing world.
They are demolished
With new structures erected.
Nineteen ninety-nine
Jack's Surfboards is still present.
But the icon
And a unique place identity
Have been effaced.
Taking their place is
Transnational architecture
Generic and inauthentic.
Is this Huntington Beach, Miami, or Montego Bay?
Is it even a place at all, or
Has it entered the realm of placelessness
With mass produced consumer products
Lining racks in a uniform mall?
A place is transformed

1. Sorkin, "Introduction," xiii.

Reflection

A sizable part of the city of Huntington Beach, California, consists of the coastal floodplain of the Santa Ana River. In the 1960s, this environment was very open. Dense fog rolled in from the ocean. Shorebirds twittered in the marshes. Frogs croaked quietly in the ponds. Farm laborers worked peacefully in agricultural fields.

But development began to spread across that flat land. Marshes were filled, agricultural fields covered. Housing tracts appeared as the residential sprawl grew, with tracts separated by long, straight streets lined with featureless block walls. As building ensued and traffic increased, urban heat grew stronger and kept the fog away. The marshes were reduced in size and bird populations declined. Agriculture began to disappear. Suburbia was encroaching.

On one hand, I feel nostalgia for the Huntington Beach of my youth. I remember riding my bike to middle school in the early morning fog, and a year or two later, biking in the pre-dawn darkness to the beach to go surfing before school. I recall the experience of nature, the sun rising as I glided through the ocean before racing to school with my hair still wet. I carry sentimental longing and wistful affection for those days in that place, perhaps even romanticizing them.

At the same time, I feel solastalgia[2] because of the erosion of my sense of belonging in that place along with a feeling of distress about the transformations that were occurring to the environment and my powerlessness to influence them. There were certainly changes to the physical environment of the place, but it

2. Albrecht, "Solastalgia," 44–59.

was alterations to the human or artificial environment that most contributed to my feelings of dislocation. The identity of the place was changing.

Before the late 1970s, Huntington Beach was a community I felt a part of because local people had created a unique place. This was especially true downtown where the surf shops sold locally-made boards and wet suits and gear, and the various other shops carried distinctive and even handcrafted cards, jewelry, and more. I moved away in 1980, in part to live in a place that matched my identity, where "landscape clues to the past"[3] were evident and I could delight in the "intimate, undisciplined, differentiation" of the place.[4] I returned to Huntington Beach in the 1990s for family reasons, to a place much different from that which I left. Gone were the marshes, the ponds, the agricultural lands, and impor-tantly, the "intimate, undisciplined, differentiation." Taking their place was a commercial culture of transnational architecture that seemed generic. It could be located anywhere. I asked myself, is this even a place at all or has it entered the realm of "placelessness,"[5] a dehumanized place with no special character?

Disappeared were the many enclaves within the landscape that brought meaning, identity, and community. The entire area seemed "commodified through neo-traditional urban design and the merchandising of local histories."[6] Names like Pacific Sands or Summerwind only served as monikers for housing tracts that were much the same.

The place I knew existed no longer. It had been supplanted.

3. Sorkin, "Introduction," xxi.
4. Sorkin, "Introduction," xiii.
5. Relph, *Place and Placelessness*.
6. Knox, "World Cities," 337.

7

Edudzinam Aklamanu

Foreseen Death

An acrid humming in the nostril,
Ignoring the signs as unreal.
Pride, hiding the damage until
Our backyards welcome the smoke ghost.
Now lost in the frightening unknown.
Clinging to the hope within our hearts,
Seeking safety in our own homes.

The only way out is through hell
As we kiss our final goodbyes.
We take the journey of no return.
As the fiery crack sings our dirge.
Our eyes dry up, mourning our fate.
The apocalypse is here.
Our judgment is near.

Reflection

"Foreseen Death" is a lament about an intense personal experience during the May 1, 2016, Fort McMurray, Alberta, fire. The powerful fire started about fifteen kilometers southwest of the city. At first, it was far enough from the town that people ignored the flames and the warnings, even though the fire was moving quickly and drawing closer to the city. It began on a normal school and workday, with families living their usual lives. I recall being aware of the fire through provincial government alerts, but it did not significantly impact me enough to warrant concern. The city had experienced minor fires here and there, and I counted this as one of them. Most of us in Fort McMurray only began to realize the gravity of the situation when the fire reached our backyards and threatened our safety. A sudden panic engulfed us when the fire swiftly spread, and we found ourselves separated from family members in other parts of the town.

In the first stanza, I describe how our pride blinded us from seeing the impending disaster. The economically driven world has reshaped our gaze and ambition in an ever-escalating pursuit of materialism, neglecting our call to follow the ways of Jesus in humility. We want things now, microwaved, and not later. We have no patience to wait for the natural process of life to evolve. This has motivated us to create remarkable inventions that meet our needs, such as heaters and air conditioners, to help ease the effects of our extreme summer and winter weather. Our inventions have helped improve lives but are also affecting the health of our planet. I believe God created the world to provide for our needs and sustain us, but with the expectation that we, as his creatures, would steward and care for what he had made. God not only created the earth for it to sustain and provide us with our nourishment, but we, in turn, have been commanded to "have dominion over the fish of the sea, over the birds of the air, and over every living thing that moves on the earth."[1] Our dominion over the earth is to be a steward of the creation and take care of it, not to abuse it.

In the second stanza, I describe the path as "hell" because we had to drive out of town with fires on each side of the road, with a feeling that we might be swallowed at any time. It was a day of fear and lament. At the end of the second stanza, I describe the Fort Mc-Murray fire as an apocalypse because that is how it felt, and it is not the only place to experience such natural disasters. All parts of the world are experiencing tragedies, ranging from floods to heat waves. These catastrophes are all signs warning us of the "foreseen death."

We need to find ways to be better prepared for natural disasters and to mitigate their causes. The Fort McMurray wildfire was a test of our readiness, which, based on my experience, we failed. I have heard from many of my Christian friends and mentors that the rise in natural disasters is a sign of the second coming of Jesus Christ, and that the only way individuals and communities can prepare for these end times is to hold on to our faith in Jesus to the end and encourage each other with the word of God. But I also know that "individuals or communities that do not adopt protective measures have less capacity to adapt to wildfire"[2] and other disasters that could be prevented if we decided to address their root causes. In Scripture, dominion is not a license for domination but a call to steward creation with love. If we are to remain faithful in times of crisis, our hope must not only look heavenward but also recognize how the choices we make on Earth impact creation and its creatures. Preparing for the return of Christ is not only about spiritual endurance but also about becoming people of integrity who protect what God has entrusted to us. We are called to watch but also to tend and restore through the way we live in a world that is groaning for healing.

1. Gen 1:28.
2. Prior and Eriksen, "Wildfire Preparedness," 1575–86.

8

Francesca Tronetti

#26

Poisons shall seep up from the river and gather in the plants
The infant shall die in its mother's womb and she will weep
She will be made barren by the food she eats and water she drinks
Her other children's skin shall blister and rash, they cry out in pain

Her husband's body shall fail him, his organs wither until his death
His seed fall dead upon his barren wife's womb without issue
His family shall be told to leave their village at once to save themselves
But where will they go with no home nor livestock to sell

The land made venomous to the man and the beast
For generations, none can live there without risk of life
Poisons still seeping up from the vast expanse of land
Casting a fog of poison to other villages.

Reflection

Growing up in Western Pennsylvania, I would travel through coal country every summer to visit my family. I saw firsthand the devastating ecological effects of mining, the slag piles still devoid of even grass long after operations had ceased. The same holds for many other mining towns in West Virginia and Wyoming. Rivers are filled with orange-red slurry, making the water toxic for both animals and humans, with no viable way to clean it up.

Pennsylvania includes the community of Donora, made infamous for a deadly smog event that killed twenty and is estimated to have injured five to seven thousand. An industrial town situated within the Allegheny Mountains, the town was often shrouded in fog, the high ridges trapping water vapor. However, an unusual weather phenomenon prevented the winds from dispersing the toxic mix of chemicals coming from the Zinc Works. Investigators found the air contained high levels of sulfur dioxide, carbon monoxide, and heavy metal dust. As broadcaster Walter Winchell reported, "People dropped dead from a thick killer fog that sickened much of the town."[1] Donora was a turning point for air pollution laws and predated the Great London smog by four years. Even as the smog persisted and ambulances reported that they could not reach the homes of those who called for help, the Zinc Works mill continued to operate, releasing more toxic fumes into the air. If the weather had not shifted, the poisonous fog could have lingered for weeks or a month.

On the other side of the United States are similar communities like Hinkley, California, made famous in the movie *Erin*

---

1. Ivory, "Murdered," 98.

Brockovich. Uncovered details about PGE Companies have revealed that they improperly stored or disposed of waste for decades, knowing that their actions were poisoning the people.[2] These were their employees, the people who did the work that generated their income, but this did not matter. Many of those affected are poor people who live in communities of color, people who cannot fight back because they don't know how or would not be listened to.

During the Flint Water Crisis of 2014, when the city water supply was switched to the heavily polluted Flint River, it took a long time for the voices of the people to be heard. Water experts and activists were ignored until Flint elected a new mayor who took their case to the federal government and the press: "When the federal state of emergency was declared, that's when the world found out that the people of Flint aren't just a bunch of crazy poor and Black folks wanting something for free. That there was actually a serious problem here."[3]

Despite an accepted legal principle, corporations are not people. While there has not been a case that explicitly states that a corporation is a person, the concept of corporate personhood has been established and upheld in the Supreme Court in some cases. The doctrine states that corporations are entitled to some of the legal rights and protections that are afforded to individuals under the law, such as the right to contribute to a political campaign.[4] They don't have children whom they want to see grow up safe and healthy, which is one of the main themes of my poetic lament. They don't have a wife who beat cancer or a brother with breathing problems. Corporations are intangible entities whose primary purpose is to generate profits for their shareholders. The people who run corporations won't always do the right thing on their own. There needs to be laws, regulations, and penalties, along with consequences for those who break them. However, the company heads and the representatives they donate to turn their workers against the agencies whose job it is to ensure the plants are

2. Ivory, "Murdered," 98.
3. DeFelicé, "10 Years After Crisis."
4. Purdue Global Law School, "Corporate Personhood."

safe. The demonization of unions as being greedy is one example. Unions were formed to protect workers from unsafe working conditions and ensure fair wages. Also, regulations and regulatory agencies have drawn the ire of some in Congress, such as Marjorie Taylor Greene.[5]

The effects of these poisons live in the land for decades, maybe even forever. Momentary greed breeds a lifetime of sorrow and pain, and in some cases, we may never fully heal the damage. So now, many US states live with barren slag piles, orange rivers, and the threat that one flood could settle the toxins in their gardens.

5. Fields, "Marjorie Taylor Greene."

9

Jane Satterfield

Emily Brontë's Advice for the Anthropocene[1]

       Haworth was a maze
of multiplying middens, mills, the pumped-up
clouds of industry, heathered moors, a haven in
a century's shrinking space. Tempting, yes,
to stick to chores, scrub the parlor carpet,
remain, in fact, remote. But as the saying goes,
there is no later. This *is* later—arctic ice melts,
shears off; strange calvings stun the circumspect
to speech. If Emily were here today,
what would she say? Though twilight calls
for a generous pour, it's better to learn dark
sonatas, the heart's own haul of grief.
The soul's compass is—or ought to be—
set straight for the storm. Some species
die without a fellow creature's comfort—
sparrows sometimes fail to thrive when solitary.
The auk's line, I've read, unraveled when stumblers
dropped the eggs. Troubadours enshrine

1. Satterfield, *Badass Brontës.*

the human truths—lies, betrayals, love
gone astray. What else would she tell us?
Aim to take dictation—a rabbit
grooming in the grass calls down the watchful hawk,
the robin's clutch in turn attracts the foraging crow.
And would we listen to her counsel
as we stand stoic in the bracing air, embrace
the static stare of endlings? *Look up*, she'd say,
you will come to call them kin.

Endling[2]

Northern white rhino: Last male Sudan dies in Kenya.[3]
—BBC NEWS, MARCH 20, 2018

Kin to the antic animal
grazing the eras of ochred lines
that roam spare grottoes, discreet
galleries, it speaks a language
guarded by gunmen—the last
of its kind in still reserve among
thickets of acacia trees. Dürer
dressed this exotic in swashbuckling
plates—a legendary likeness of Coliseum
combat. From our vantage of close-up
lenses, of flickering screens, this beast is
wide-muzzled, all bristly hide, gaze trained
low on grassland to roam by day and
up to half the night. Another click offers
up a cache of tagged, poached horn—
hoarded for elixirs and curatives—
a planet's digitized requiem. O wallower,
pale warship in silty water holes,
linger a while beneath Kilimanjaro's
visible enchantment of snow, O face
caught in the crosshairs of going and gone.

2. Satterfield, "Endling."
3. BBC News, "Northern White Rhino."

Reflection

In *Learning to Die in the Anthropocene: Reflections on the End of Civilization*, journalist Roy Scranton considers the effects of global climate change and the attendant prospect of social collapse. Adjusting to this new order, he observes, will require "more than scientific data and military policy." Instead, Scranton advocates that we develop "new myths and stories" to foster "a new relationship to the deep polyglot tradition of human culture that carbon-based capitalism has vitiated through commodification and assimilation."[4] Creative writers in all genres are increasingly responding to this call by documenting—through varied perspectives and genres—the personal and generational impact of climate change in order to spark the imaginative empathy that leads to social change and committed environmental stewardship.

The writing of laments, I feel, is a necessary contribution to this genre. Wherever we write and read—in the quiet of a school room or home studio, amid the clatter of a local coffee shop or subway platform, or in the cool green of a public park—poetry's origins as an oral tradition, with its power to mourn and heal, is within reach. My own poems take their cue from firsthand observations of the creatures who inhabit my own ecotone, as well as written accounts in public forums. They also draw on the influence of an important predecessor—Victorian poet and novelist Emily Brontë (1818–1848)—a proto-environmentalist who acted as occasional wildlife rescuer and wrote powerfully about the Yorkshire moors. Yorkshire, though geographically remote, was, in Brontë's time, home to the textile mills and crowded settlements in which

4. Scranton, *Learning to Die*, 19.

she witnessed the troubling effects of human encroachment and industrialization. Brontë's poetic vision encompasses a view of nature that recognized the impending threat and celebrated the danger and beauty implicit in creation, as well as pointing out human cruelties that perpetuate social injustice, violence, and war.

With limited formal education and lifetimes most spent in the isolation of their father's parsonage, sisters Charlotte, Emily, and Anne were deeply immersed in the history and politics of their time. The 1801 Enclosure Act had abolished the system of open agriculture and ownership of common lands. The textile mills and crowded settlements of the Brontës' remote Yorkshire landscape brought the troubling effects of human encroachment and industrialization. As children, Anne and Emily witnessed an historic bog burst that sent a seven-foot-high tide of mud into the air—an event well-documented in local papers of the day. The Crow Hill Bog Burst is now viewed by researchers as a sign of environmental distress that speaks to the challenge of pinpointing the onset of the Anthropocene.[5] The work of Emily and her sisters possesses a deep attention to place and the natural world consistent with the Victorian tradition of botanizing, or close study of plants and animals in a given locale. "High Waving Heather," composed on December 13, 1836, captures Emily's response to the winter landscape whose beauty withstands seasonal storms and inspires divine reverence. Beyond the realm of scholars and literary readers, Emily's poems live on, in part, because of their visionary scope, environmental acuity, and striking musicality—qualities captured in recent song cycles by recording artists that include Swedish folk singer Sofie Livebrant and The Unthanks, Yorkshire-based folk artists who include sisters Rachel and Becky Unthank. Noteworthily, the group's settings of Emily's texts were performed on Emily's piano in the Brontë Parsonage Museum.[6]

"Emily Brontë's Advice for the Anthropocene" considers which perspectives Brontë's naturalistic vision might offer those living in the era of the Sixth Extinction, a time where human

5. Ross, *Charlotte Brontë*, 4–5.
6. Unthanks, "Lines—Part Three—Emily Brontë."

activity has caused mass extinction at a rate that may soon wipe out up to half of all living species. Faced with our own era's environmental challenges, what counsel would she offer? Haworth, as many readers may know, is the village that shaped the Brontë family's daily life, its tempting natural prospect and inspiring landscapes under constant threat of a changing world in which a dehumanizing mechanization alarmed the sensibilities of the literary sisters. In my poem, Emily's sympathies with the living world find expression in the knowledge not available to her then, in part because the unfolding of future extinctions and their global acceleration were not yet underway. For example, Emily refers to reading about the auk's threatened lineage, but that memory is, in fact, my own—one I felt would fit Emily's own concerns about both nonhuman life and the need to give them shelter. As my fictionalized Emily observes, in recommending that we empathize with our fellow creatures' plight, "Look up . . . you will come to call them kin."

"Endling" mourns the death of Sudan, the last male Northern white rhino in Kenya, who lived out his final days in a sanctuary guarded by armed keepers—an image that documents the stark reality of species loss that has been driven by illegal global trade. Particularly painful is the thought that these strangely majestic creatures, "wide-muzzled all bristly hide," could be treated as some sort of unfeeling, non-sentient natural resource—like the soil or mountainsides that themselves have so often been criminally mutilated by the mining industries and the legacy of extractive economies that continue shape our lives. It's almost as if the rhinos' very solidness, its muscle and heft, its armored hide—suggest it is unliving and therefore ripe for exploitation and abuse: "another click offers / up a cache of tagged, poached horn—horded for elixirs and curatives." (How tragic that living endling's death should be perceived as medicinal by humankind). The image of Sudan the rhino carried all this and more; I was struck and saddened by the contrast between his image and prehistoric representations of ancient rhinos (such as those painted on cave walls in Chauvet Cave, Ardeche, France, or those etched onto rocks in South Africa).

Though the origins and ritual significance of these images is lost to history, the artwork is a powerful reminder of our own passing through geological time; it extends our kinship with distant ancestors whose responses to their environment are rendered with beauty and awe.

For me, laments are never expressions of defeat but expressions of sorrow that are both cathartic and a call to action. Action always begins with changing people's minds, expanding their awareness, or nudging them to become more acutely aware of something they already know. In these poems and other environmentally focused works, I write against an awareness of human encroachment and the deleterious effects of climate crisis, with the hopes that documentation of grief may offer healing and possibly inspire action born of love for a more-than-human world.

10

Jeremiah Bašurić

A Cry, a Question, a Tanaga

The day we denied Earth's life:
The day we denied our own.
God's image shatters in strife
Christ's blood spills on floors, my home,
Along with children of God.
Sacred blood soaks sacred land
Thick. This lush system we trod
Blind to the red on each hand.

How long, O Lord, will You bleed?
Whence endless store does life come?
How much longer do You need?
To finish what will be done.
"Strange providence" it may be
Or Your sardonic pleasure.
Torn flesh—aching to be free
Or submits without measure.

JEREMIAH BAŠURIĆ

Can we see life in the earth
Again? See *Thy will* anew?
Our denial turn to mirth?
Your image reflect what's true?
How long, O Lord, will You bleed?
Whence endless store does love come?
Avenge the earth! Strike that greed.
Forgive weak bodies undone.

55

Reflection

The above variation of a Filipino *Tanaga* is a lament over the plague of whiteness covering the earth. Whiteness, as described by Willie Jennings, is a diseased theological imagination that has infected hearts, minds, and bodies of the lands ravaged by colonization. In his important work *The Christian Imagination: Theology and The Origins of Race* (2011), Jennings argues, "The deepest theological distortion taking place is that the earth, the ground, spaces and places are being removed as living organizers of identity and as facilitators of identity."[1] This distortion is an essential component of whiteness. Jennings' chapter in a book of the same name, "Can White People be Saved?" argues that "whiteness as a way of being in the world has been parasitically joined to a Christianity that is also a way of being in the world. It was the fusion of these two realities that gave tragic shape to Christian faith in the New World."[2]

Instead of imagining the land, animals, and humanity as intimately connected and mutually bound, as many Indigenous communities understand it, Jennings argues that Christian colonists enacted a "revolt against creation."[3] They claimed to be persons at the center of reality, able to project meaning onto the land: "we interpret and manipulate the world as we see fit, taking from it what we need, and caring for it within the logics of making it more productive for us; that is, we draw the world to its proper fulfillment."[4] Humanity became owners of the land rather than "being owned

1. Jennings, *Christian Imagination*, 39.
2. Jennings, *Can "White" People Be Saved?*, 27.
3. Jennings, *Christian Imagination*, 248.
4. Jennings, *Can "White" People Be Saved?*, 32.

by the land" in a reciprocal relationship.[5] Thankfully, my own relationship to the land remedied this plague to some extent. My biracial family was *owned* by an acreage in rural Alberta. Since we did not have much material wealth, we relied on the land. For me, the prairie sunsets, the golden crops, the Canadian geese overhead proclaimed the sacred life of creation, of a life I was intrinsically part of. Feeling the life of a ram leaving its body as I struggled to hold it down and seeing its blood soak into the sacred ground left a spiritual impression. I sensed that I was naturally part of the prairie landscape—not a detached soul extracting from the earth. For most of my childhood, I actually felt more comfortable defecating in the woods. I revolted against my mother when she scolded me for sneaking a roll of toilet paper outside to do my business.

At the same time, I was far from immune to the plague of whiteness. I was blind to the implications of its distortion, especially in regard to the peoples the Creator had first nursed on this land. Jennings argues that not only did the land suffer from this new imagination, but humanity did as well. The land and human bodies were seen as things to be controlled and manipulated for a determined commercial end. In this perverse and deformed view of maturity, humans could move from being *owned* like the land to becoming an *owner* of the land. Of course, this maturity was also dependent on your initial value. Like land, value was determined through enclosure and then commodification, so humans were forced into "racial encasement," which made it easier for one to determine one's place in the spectrum of *owned* to *owner*.[6] Another dimension of this deformed maturity was born: from *darkness* to whiteness. Black and brown bodies were slaves to the colony and lighter bodies were, essentially, its indentured servants. Those who become owners of the land (and bodies) were considered great in the kingdom. This also set the stage of one's path from *stranger* to *citizen*. Immigrants coming to the new world attempted to overcome their strangeness—and the accompanying vulnerability—by forming the land into their own image. They engaged in "taming

5. Jennings, *Can "White" People Be Saved?*, 37.

6. Jennings, *Can "White" People Be Saved?*, 31.

the land" through fragmentation. It was a kind of organization that shattered and divided parts rather than bringing them in harmony together. To do this, they simultaneously placed their "bodies in the unfolding drama of destroying the Native inhabitants" and stripped away their former, *immature* identities to make way for citizenship in a new, more evolved world.[7] Jennings argues that, as fragmentation increased, borders became more pronounced, as did nationalism. Jennings says, "Conversion to the faith has been brought inside the cultivating work of turning immigrants into citizens. Christianity indeed makes good citizens."[8] In this matrix, "Native bodies were perceived as closer to nature and its raw condition of unproductivity, of potentiality, yet to be realized."[9]

By the time my parents immigrated to Canada, the land was already fragmented. The straight lines and fences defining the *useful* from wild land; the *habitable* from inhabitable shelter; the *enlightened* humans from commodified nature had already been set and its grid, like a net, wrapped around my heart and mind. My father, in particular, tried to tame the land into his own image. Though it was an image very different from the colonists before him—our home was called by the bullies on the yellow school bus the "dirty farm"—it also did not diverge far in other respects, especially in regards to Indigenous people. Although we did have a few Indigenous friends nearby, we also participated in many dehumanizing jokes and comments at their expense. In our mind, Indigenous peoples were akin to the wild, unproductive land or disobedient goat. They needed more growth, maturity, progress. They ought to be good citizens of this good Christian country like we were becoming.

That net, which entangled me, was slowly cut away in university. There, the deformed maturity from *owned* to *owner* was subverted through my environmental studies degree; from *darkness* to *whiteness* was challenged through theological studies focusing on God's shalom and jubilee; from *stranger* to *citizen* was

7. Jennings, Can "White" People Be Saved?, 36.

8. Jennings, Can "White" People Be Saved?, 38.

9. Jennings, Can "White" People Be Saved?, 39.

debunked while living amongst two First Nations communities. As my knowledge increased concerning the extent of this plague, so did my sorrow. Grief and weariness grew as I communed with children of God experiencing poverty, homelessness, and injustice. I became angry at people who closely resembled whiteness. I was angry at God, who allowed it to happen.

In my studies, I recently came across a Mohegan preacher named Samson Occom. He thoroughly resisted this plague of whiteness even as it gobbled up the land and his people. In the midst of this plague, Occom believed that God in Christ Jesus, the providential one, was with his people amid their despair and suffering. By some extraordinary faith, he believed that colonization was somehow part of the "strange providence" of God, who made him both Indigenous and a Christian.[10] Occom's words, wisdom, and resistance allowed me to breathe again. I lament not to some void or empty space but to the Spirit of Christ, who is my hope, who hears us, who bleeds with creation.

10. Brooks and Clayton, *American Lazarus*, 84.

11

Joanne M. Moyer

A Lament Inspired by Genesis 1–3; Psalm 96, 97, 104; Isaiah 55; Jeremiah 4; Hosea 4; Romans 8; and the Planetary Boundaries

One: In the beginning, God created the heavens and the earth.
        And God declared creation good.

Many: It was very good!

One: All creation sang with joy!
        Then sin entered the world,
        And Eden's gates were closed.
        Creation's singing changed to groaning,
        As gardens turned to desolation,
        And fruitful land became desert.

Many: The earth mourns.
        We mourn with it.
        Lord, have mercy.

One: Trees no longer clap their hands,
        Their branches cut,
        Deep roots unearthed,
        Birds have no place to build their nests.

JOANNE M. MOYER

Many: The land mourns.
We mourn with it.
Lord, have mercy.

One: Gushing springs are dammed and clogged,
Clear waters tainted,
The thirsty go unquenched.

Many: The earth mourns.
We mourn with it.
Lord, have mercy.

One: Land and sky once teemed with life.
Passenger pigeons filled the skies.
Wild bison covered the plains.
Now they are gone.
Monarch butterflies search for food
And find only poison.

Many: The land mourns.
We mourn with it.
Lord, have mercy.

One: Seasons have lost their rhythm.
Raging storms wash our homes away,
Farmland parches in drought.

Many: The earth mourns.
We mourn with it.
Lord, have mercy.

One: Air is filled with smoke and ash,
All who breathe it choke.

Many: The land mourns.
We mourn with it.
Lord, have mercy.

One: Coral reefs are bleaching,
Fish have no place to rest.
Fishers come home with empty nets.

Many: The earth mourns.
We mourn with it.
Lord, have mercy.

One: Over all the earth, God's creation languishes:
        The mountains and the trees,
        The cattle of the fields and the birds of air,
        The wild animals and the fish of the seas.
        All creation groans,
        Waiting with eager longing to be set free,
        From its bondage of decay.

Many: The land mourns.
        We mourn with it.
        Lord, have mercy.

Reflection

In the winter of 2024, I was asked by a pastor friend to run a weekend retreat at his church about creation care. The weekend ended with a Sunday morning worship service, which he and I planned together. We structured the service as a series of readings and songs, starting with praise and thanksgiving, rooting ourselves in the gifts and beauty of creation, then moved into confession, action response, and finally, hope. Before entering the challenge of confession and action, I wanted a lament that would allow us to sit in sadness, without pointing fingers of blame or thinking about what needed to be done. It felt like an important emotional step to just spend some time being sad about all wounds of this beautiful world before moving into pieces that assigned responsibility. But in searching worship resources, I couldn't find anything that did this. All the readings I found brought confession of sin into the lament almost immediately. My friend tried to write something, but it didn't quite accomplish what I was hoping, so when I was asked to run the retreat again later that spring, I sat down and wrote this lament.

Since I had been using the planetary boundaries as a framework to illustrate global ecological realities during the retreat, I tried to reference each of the boundaries in my lament. The Planetary Boundaries were developed by scientists at the Stockholm Resilience Center to identify the key planetary systems that are essential to life on Earth, and to track how human activity is affecting these systems.[1] They include biosphere integrity, the well-being of living creatures and the diversity of ecosystems, measured

---

1. Stockholm Resilience Centre, "Planetary Boundaries."

by species variety, genetic diversity, and the functional services creatures provide, such as photosynthesis and pollination.

They also include climate change, which refers to overall planetary heating and extreme weather events caused primarily by the burning of fossil fuels; ocean acidification, the absorption of atmospheric carbon dioxide that forms carbonic acid and disrupts marine life; and land-system change, including deforestation, desertification, and the conversion of natural spaces into cities and farmland. In their most recent analysis, scientists determined that all but three of these systems (ocean acidification, atmospheric aerosol loading, and stratospheric ozone depletion) have exceeded the boundaries determined as safe zones for life on Earth. Ocean acidification and atmospheric aerosols are creeping closer to those boundaries, while stratospheric ozone depletion has improved in the last decades and is the only Planetary Boundary I did not include in my lament.

This second retreat took place in Alberta, so I tried to include examples from our local ecosystems, such as the bison, which used to cover the landscape where we live, and the wildfire smoke, which we have experienced in recent summers. I also intentionally wrote about both impacts that affect humans and impacts that affect other living creatures on Earth. As I wove these examples into my lament, I borrowed words from the Bible, from the Genesis creation stories, psalms that praise God's creation, and passages that talk about how the land is affected by sin: "the earth shall mourn" (Jer 4:28); "the land mourns" (Hos 4:3); and "the whole creation has been groaning" (Rom 8:22). I wanted the words I used to sound familiar, be rooted in the tradition of the people who were saying them, and resonate at the core of their faith. This lament is intended to be spoken aloud as a collective.

12

Justin Dodd Mullikin

The Old Farmers

1

As a child in Kentucky,
I sat on the side of a tobacco field
with my dad, in the shade.
Hot from the work, and a little old,
he tried to doze.
Still enchanted with the world, and young,
I asked questions.

. . .

"Dad, what's this plant called?"
I asked.
That's ragweed; what makes you sneeze.
So, I don't like it much,
but something's got to.
The Good Lord wouldn't put it here
for no reason.

"Why don't you cut all the weeds down?"
I asked.
Son, a weed's just a plant
people think is useless or ugly.
But if we cut all this down,
what would the deer eat?
Where would the rabbits hide?
"What was here before the weeds and tobacco?"
I asked.
It was all forest,
as far as you could see.
Used to be, a squirrel could travel
from the ocean to the Mississippi
and never once touch the ground.
"Is it fun, being a farmer?"
I asked.
You do what you like, but truth is
it's getting hard.
I'm the only full-time farmer out here now.
Too much work for too little money.
But I like it; that's all I know.

2

As an adult, living in Rwanda,
I sat on the side of a maize field
talking with elderly farmers.
Curious about this outsider, or out of politeness,
they talked.
Curious about their work, and how things had changed,
I asked questions.

. . .

"I heard there are different names for the soil.
What's this one called?"
I asked.

Gitwa is like this place where we are sitting.
It is soil that produces more
than all other types of soil.
Gitwa has a beautiful black color, and it is soft, too.
There is *rwona*, the soil that doesn't yield,
and *amayaga*, which doesn't produce much.
And another one is called *indeka*,
which is the one that yields more.
Munyere is that soil that is red.
If you plant there without any fertilizer,
the maize will sprout with red leaves.
Ikidudu is soil where cows used to be around;
where the log fire would be lit,
and where they would rest.
Ikidudu doesn't need fertilizers.
Because it contains very old manure.
That soil in which you plant maize and it sprouts
in the blink of eye, looking nice.
"What used to be here before the farms?"
I asked.
There were trees.
There were those called
ndakatsi, intusi, sipure, and so on.
And nowadays, coffee.
You just see coffee trees.

3

"Do your children know all of this?"
I asked.
How can they know?
They only know what they study at school,
modern music, politics, and nothing else.
There were many traditions related to agriculture,
which are dying off nowadays.
They live in different worlds;
as we can't know the modern ones,

so they can't know the past ones.
We don't have any scholar knowledge;
we only know the hoe.
So for us, even as we work,
we work for our children.
"Do you want your children to be farmers?"
I asked.
I hope they can be something else.
Farming is getting too hard now.
Rains never come on time and there is too much sun.
No, only if there is nothing else
can I want them to be a farmer.
What I can add is that in the past
crops would grow, no problem.
But nowadays . . .
I don't know what happened to the soil.
It got depleted.
The earth is old.
Nowadays, you have to force the soil.
People also loved each other back then;
they knew the value of a person, more than today.
You used to prepare sorghum beer,
and invite people to come and help you farm.
After the work was done, you would go drink,
eat, sing, and dance until it's finished,
and go back to your homes happy.

4

They are just working to get money now.
They don't have that time to dance;
they are only focused on cultivating.
There are even those who are more advanced,
who are using machines to farm!
And can the machines dance?!
No . . . Our culture is dying.

. . .

I told them about our farm and my dad,
the last real farmer he knew.
And together we sat in nostalgia
and grief
over all the things lost
and the lost names of things we still see
but no longer *know*.

Reflection

I grew up on a tobacco farm in Kentucky and, by the time I was in college, my dad was the last of our neighbors farming full-time. As a child, our family and neighbors would all pitch in to start the season's tobacco crop, look for lost cattle, or bring in the hay. Over time, however, as people steadily left our farming community, my father found it increasingly difficult to keep things going. He couldn't make enough money to hire the necessary labor and eventually had to sell off a large portion of the farm. He grew his last crop of tobacco in the summer of 2014 and missed farming dearly. Some of the last stories he told before he died in February of 2024 were about working tobacco. The first section of my lament is an amalgamation of the many conversations I had with my dad when I was young and spent every summer working with him in the fields.

After college, I got a job in Rwanda working on an agricultural development project. After experiencing my father's struggle to make a viable livelihood from agriculture, I was intensely curious about how other people, in other places, went about farming. I lived and worked in Rwanda for nearly a decade and, through countless conversations with farmers, realized that many of their narratives mirrored my father's: historically and culturally important crops, such as sorghum, were disappearing and, along with them, the attendant rituals, place-based knowledges, and labor practices that sustain a community. I received my PhD in geography from Rutgers University in 2023 with a dissertation on agrarian change in Rwanda. The second section of my lament is comprised of quotations from interviews and focus groups with dozens of farmers in eastern Rwanda from 2019 to 2020, lightly edited for this format and reimagined as one conversation.

The agricultural "modernization" policies being implemented in Rwanda and across the globe aim to transform farming from a custodial act of mutual reproduction into an extractive business of linear production. This is not a new phenomenon; the present forms, actors, and rationales driving these changes are a patina on the racialized, capitalist-colonial origins of the tobacco and coffee plantations that violently extracted profit through the conquest and dispossession of land, and through enslavement or taking of human life.[1] Tobacco and coffee both, however, in a tragic historical irony, were not grown by Indigenous people in the United States and Sub-Saharan Africa for hundreds of years. In fact, before the crops were commodified, the locations were considered *sacred*. As bell hooks once observed, the near-wholesale commodification of this affective relationship between land and people "severs tobacco from its roots as a healing and sacred plant. Just as the colonization of Native and African people required that they be stripped of their language, identity, and dehumanized, the tobacco plant underwent a similar process."[2]

This type of deeply impactful human-nature relationship is a function of agrarianism itself; farmers were *cultivating, raising,* and practicing *husbandry* long before they were "producing" anything. After all, "the produce of a farm is neither made nor found—but *grown*."[3] To maintain a pastoral, cultural, or even spiritual connection to these cash crops—as my father did with tobacco and as many Rwandan farmers do with any number of crops that have been captured by the market—is not to sanction or excuse their recent, violent histories, but to reclaim a more autochthonous relationship with(in) the more-than-human world.

The same extractive logic drives global climate change: the ever-expanding commodification and exploitation of humans and nonhuman natures, divorced from *place* and stripped of affective

---

1. Wynter, "Novel and History," 95–102.
2. hooks, *Belonging*, 111.
3. Singh, "Affective Labor of Growing Forests," 192.

meaning, primarily in service of profit and power. Much of my research in Rwanda centered around the disappearance of folk songs and poems that celebrated specific crops, such as sorghum, that had been central to the agrarian economy and culture for centuries before being supplanted by cash crops. When asked about the differences between these agrarian songs of the past and those of today, one farmer said to me,

> Now when a person makes a song . . . the song conveys growing a lot of that crop, so as to harvest a lot of it, get a lot of money, and even export it and such other stuff. . . . [In the past] those sweet potatoes, that sorghum, those beans, they would stay where they were grown. They would be eaten there, or [used] there. But today, taking maize as an example, it is grown and then it is delivered to different provinces in the country, and even abroad. So, the artist who makes the song will show that that crop earns money. That is the difference.[4]

During my research in Rwanda, many older farmers expressed nostalgia over their communities' "loss of love" as rapid socio-ecological change forced people into precarious market production or off the land entirely. As Wendell Berry has written, "people *exploit* what they have merely concluded to be of value, but they *defend* what they love. To defend what we love we need a particularizing language, for we love what we particularly know."[5] This means cultivating a nurturing relationship with the land, the crops, and the soils, beyond their market value; knowing all of their uses and limitations and their names is an act of love, and a defense of communities that prioritize stewardship and reciprocity over profit and extraction.

I wrote this lament not only for the ongoing ecological destruction of climate change but also for the ongoing loss of knowledges, communities, and ways of being with and in the world; I wrote it for the plants, the soils, the landscapes, and all human and more-than-human natures that we can no longer love because

---

4. Farmer, personal communication, 2020.

5. Berry, *Life Is a Miracle*, 41.

we no longer have a mutually *re*productive relationship with. As a result, we pass on to our children not only a dangerously uncertain future but diminishing opportunities to know and love the world.

13

Liana DePoe-Rix

This is a trigger warning before my chapter, which deals with themes of sexual assault and suicidality. If this is going to be difficult, please skip ahead and be gentle with yourself!

Small

Hear each hollow footfall on the living earth
Each rippling raindrop on the silent water's surface and
Each victorious note of birdsong that defies the quiet.

I am so, so small

Fading quicker than each ripple of the rain
Into the reflections of the towering trees and mountains that watch
patiently, benevolently,
Lovingly—as alive as I—
Each tiny, billowing wave that comes of my flailing,
My grasping wildly at this wild
As if it wasn't already between my fingertips
As if what lays unbridled beneath the still surface does not lie in
wait between each beat of my heart as it aches

Miniscule ripples, still seen, still felt,
Still—known

Although the ripples fade, they still were

hazy clarity

a year
a notebook I swore I'd've filled
by now—boxed up neatly next to my trauma
and my thoughts of back then—
but those memories do not take well
to being pushed aside—
of when my brain was set to broil
bubbling with unending thoughts and toil
I've written a fraction of the feeling—steaming—
but I've realized I'll never fully capture the reeling
the roiling storm of my mind
pulled back
lightning-struck blazes now
reduced
to the haze that hangs lazily in each breath
I exhale
this tiny pocket-sized book, not even half finished,
returns diminished,
and here I thought the poems would
make the pain worth it

but as I try to bask in the stillness,
and settle,
listening to the smoke,
an echo of the flame,
I think the pain is just pain
and that letting myself feel it—

Grieve
watching the silver flash of fish
as they break the glass surface
of the water to
feed—
that the pain is far from
everything—

reflecting
I sit, a pilgrim,
amongst the insects and the minnows
that cautiously
inspect me—
now that I'm still
enough to blend in
as one of their own,
just another hot-blooded mammal
incomplete
yet whole
Enough.

On Pyramid Lake (from Afar)

I don't know the scope of what remains
through the snow and the smoke
I have been changed
Irrevocably
as has the land
that cradled me
though this haze is now familiar
I still can't quite see clearly

but I'm getting better at seeing the flickering shapes
and patterns they inhabit

this
crook
ed
twisting of our planet

All I know is that I love—
I love
I love
I love
deeply enough that I stayed
to see what sprouts from the ashes

the cicatrice that stitches
me
or is it

Us?
back together
but not into what I was
or what that place was either

something new
I can only hope it's something better
but to say that feels like a disservice to
all my chronic reminders
of what I used to be able to do
(believe)
(the person I tried to be)
(the world I thought I lived in)

so I'll fill the last few pages
of this meek little pocket of time
with my meager attempt to capture
that while I know I could be better (the world that could be better)
I'm okay—I'm still breathing
and I'm still so fucking small
and that's a relief just as much as it is a burden
the words still flow—
I filled the pages
(even if it wasn't as fast or as eloquent as I might've liked)

the burnt mountains are still standing
the lake still ripples when the rain brings the fires to a fizzle
three years
and three thousand years in the future
to live is to change
to grow to hurt
to listen and be listened to
and to love
and love
and love
What little time we have on Earth!

So I'll fight back my cynicism enough to say
that while it's true we need our grief
it isn't an option to admit defeat—
most of the things that we can help
are within arm's reach
I don't have the power to stop a billionaire from dumping oil into
the sea
but I can point him out to the person beside me, and hopefully,
they'll do the same
people are never one—we're many
I can't end all violence against the vulnerable
but I can listen to them the way I wish someone listened to me
and believe
humans are a communal species,
an emotional animal of which no one is truly independent of the
other
I don't have the answers
And I don't think I ever will
But I'll try to parse the patterns hopefully
Interrupt what needs interrupting, and let the rest be
keep traveling to where I can let it all sit with me
the ocean, the mountains—
Anywhere with trees
(the branches outside my window are still swaying in the breeze as
they have since I was a child)
breathe
let the air fill my lungs and accept what it contains
and give my broken heart a chance to beat

Reflection

In 2022, I was on Dr. Ferber's Geography class trip to Jasper, Alberta, and wrote a poem during our reflection time at Pyramid Lake. It was a grey, overcast morning, and a steady drizzle had settled over us as we made our way across the bridge and then dispersed for some quiet time for individual reflection. Around that time, I had been subconsciously avoiding introspection, but with no other choice but to reflect inwardly, I was surprised by what was drawn out of me. I watched the rain kiss the surface of the water and did something that I still don't love to do, no matter how necessary and unavoidable it may be: let myself feel my pain.

I've always considered myself a poet, and I've always loved to read poetry, but at that time, I'd felt pretty cut off artistically. I'd given myself over to a degree of numbness for self-protection, which isn't the greatest practice for mental health or artistic expression. But as I sat there, I felt the need to write a poem—an urge that hadn't taken hold of me for months and was sorely missed. I think it's impossible to distill raw feeling into words entirely, but I think that art gives us our best shot at getting our point across. I tapped the raw words into my phone screen as I wiped away the gentle raindrops, embracing the cool morning air against my skin.

I initially presented the "small" poem as about grief in general, as there is a distinct feeling of helplessness that comes with mourning. We can only do so much—and in the grand scheme of things, it can feel like nothing we do as individuals will ever be enough. Be it a personal grief—like the illness of a loved one—or a larger scale anxiety, like the state of the environment on our planet or the governments that rule it. We have so little control over so much that affects us, and sometimes, for me at least, this leads to despair.

For me, though, the grief ran a bit deeper in ways I wasn't comfortable putting into explicit prose at the time (hence the poetry). I had been a victim of sexual violence the year of this class trip and hadn't yet fully processed the extent of the effect the trauma had had on me. I'd just barely admitted what had happened to myself, let alone anybody else.

This small poem represented the opening of the floodgates of poetry for me again, after it had been on a shelf for a while and only brushed off when I had to write poetry for class. I was writing for myself again, plus it was being encouraged. I steeled myself and read my poem to the class, and it was received far better than I ever would've imagined it would. The encouragement made me pick up a little pocket-sized notebook from a gift shop with the intention of filling the pages with poetry.

And to my own surprise as I write this, I have.

Not nearly as quickly as I planned, mind you; it took three years of keeping that tiny book in my purse and a bit of duct tape to keep it intact, but I did. I ended up failing the Geography course the first time before taking it again a year later. Going on the Jasper trip again provided a very poignant marker for how far I'd come, and how far yet I had to go in terms of recovery. I brought along that little book from the year prior, and as I sat at Pyramid Lake again, on a much sunnier, albeit smokier day, I climbed out to a rock in the water so I could be surrounded by the reflection of the smoky sky above me and did one of my favorite things to do in large bodies of water: keep as still as possible and wait for the fish to come back, and they did. The minnows returned to inspect my shoes as they sat submerged in the water and now a part of their scenery, and I let myself reflect on my imperfect progress.

This was the summer of 2023, when the Jasper area was ravaged by wildfires, and I couldn't help the morbid thought of how the smoke in the sky was much akin to how what I'd experienced still hung over me. How no amount of healing will erase the fact that I was wounded in the first place. The same can be said for our planet. The earth will survive, but humans have changed this planet in a way that cannot be reversed.

For better or for worse.

It feels strange to reflect on that time while I write this in 2025 because the fires to come the following summer were so much more violent and consumed so much more. Sometimes, I feel like our world is becoming scarier each passing year, both environmentally and politically. Existing as a queer person in Alberta doesn't always feel safe, and then I think about how much I care about the environment and wonder if any human will feel safe in a few decades because of what we've done to our planet.

I seem to cling to this idea that we need to care about everything all the time—social media has certainly not helped on this front. Constant exposure to an overwhelming amount of news can just lead to you feeling as though anything you, as one individual, can do won't matter in the long run. Thus, that feeling of helplessness seeps in, and for me, at least, that feeling of helplessness is more painful than any grief. Sometimes, I find myself lost in a whirlwind of tragedy, with so many things to be upset about that I don't even know where to begin.

But anxiety is not activism. Though our hearts may ache for what we cannot help, we mustn't live in that state of mourning constantly. It's important to feel that sadness, yes, because to ignore it, to shove that feeling aside is to do ourselves an immense disservice, and sorrow has a way of creeping back up on us when we try to avoid it, anyway.

Feelings demand to be felt.

Once we've done our part, that's all we can do, and however small a part yours may be, I assure you that it matters. The effort matters. The things you can have an impact on are often right in front of you, whether that's going out of your way to make the queer people in your life feel safer, educating yourself on social issues, protesting policies that threaten the safety of our planet and the people living on it, or picking up litter at your local park.

I've learned to embrace when things don't go according to plan. I didn't pass Geography on the first try, I didn't fill up my poetry notebook with the fervor I'd expected from myself. But I did pass Geography the second time, and I did fill up my poetry notebook. I didn't kill myself, even when some days it was all I wanted to do.

It just took some time and a few tries, and the trying is the part that matters.

14

Lori Matties

fall

spring trees moan a windy paean of praise
to seeds, soil, deep down creatures
who nourish them,
to water seeping upward

but a woman stands in the boulevard
arms encircling an old elm
marked with the city's orange dot of death

summer conifers are browning
worry lines etch the
wrinkling face of earth

september rains too much

untimely october snow
weighs heavy on dry branches
still adorned with leaves
the crack and slash of limbs

Climate of Lament

create a war zone
of grief

restless december trees write a dirge on the sky
to their dying ones
tired lungs exhale

breathe on me, breath of God
fill me with life anew
that I may love what thou dost love
and do what thou wouldst do[1]

---

1. Hatch, "Breathe on Me."

Birdbath (Spring 2021)

blue jay perches
preening at the bowl's edge
throat vibrating as it swallows
and surveys
steeling its glittering eyes at all comers

the garrulous sparrows who wintered here became my friends—
        spruce condominia
        are shelter and choir loft, courtroom
        of not so civil suits

blue jay with crested wedgewood beauty
shrills like a hawk

attests that I also have cracked and creased
the ground, felled and burned
those who give me breath

the house in which I've wintered
has been wrested from some other birdcity,
and mined from innocent stones

let blue jay school me, then

I have forgotten for so long
how my kind
eats birds for breakfast

lament for the death of wonder

when wonder died
no New Orleans jazz band
bleated the beat down the street
nor solemn bagpipes
blew a windy dirge
to summon anyone's attention.
no one Googled "when did wonder die?"

wonder's deflated sails
hung limp on a dry desultory day.
she just lay down
while her children marched
to work like so many ants
going down
to the earth
to get out
of the rain

the rain falls
like leaves in the forest
drifting lonely
to the grieving ground

say

say you saw creation
lying beaten and bruised
by the side of the road

maybe the neighborly thing
would be to sit down beside her and weep

love wears a face,
be it furred or leafy
or full of beak,
and maybe creation could use
a donkey, an inn, or a few coins
to tide her over
till you can return
to pay in full

Reflection

I live in Winnipeg, Manitoba, where winters are long and summers are glorious. We share a big sky with the prairie provinces west of us. Nuances of flat and rolling landforms are not lost on our sense of prairie beauty. As one who grew up in Edmonton, I am a city person, but I have spent my summers by Lake Wabamun, eighty kilometers (fifty miles) west of the city, wandering the ferny forest and collecting wild berries.

A report by the Government of Canada and the three prairie provinces states that summers are growing longer, warmer, and drier, storms more intense.[2] Forest fires and floods are more frequent. Exotic weeds are moving in. Winters are shorter, less cold, and wetter, except for 2021 to 2022, which was colder, longer, and snowier than usual. Ironically, when I started this reflection in June 2022, Manitoba was experiencing the second wettest spring on record.

The poems I offer here are part of an ongoing series that documents how changing weather and human industry are affecting the more-than-human beings in my Winnipeg neighborhood; those who cannot speak in language we humans readily understand. I grieve over how we have failed to pay attention. And I try to let the creatures teach me how to be a better citizen of Earth, a better tender and protector of all that God has created, a partner in the community of creation.

The poem "fall" observes a year of stress and damage to the trees in and around the city. Winnipeg is known for its lush urban forest, yet every year, more centenarian trees are cut down

2. ClimateWest, *State of the Climate Report.*

because of Dutch Elm disease. City planners who planted these beautiful trees a hundred years ago had not learned to consider how a mono crop of non-native trees would fare. When the trees began to die, they planted Ash trees, which now are under threat from the Emerald Ash borer. An unseasonal snowstorm in October 2019 caused heavy damage to trees that could not withstand the weight of wet snow on branches that were still full of leaves. Drought across the prairies has weakened the trees further. Recent work by scientists such as Suzanne Simard has shown us the intelligence and cooperation of trees:

> [Trees] are in a web of interdependence, linked by a system of underground channels, where they perceive and connect and relate with an ancient intricacy and wisdom that can no longer be denied. I conducted hundreds of experiments, with one discovery leading to the next, and through this quest I uncovered the lessons of tree-to-tree communication, of the relationships that create a forest society.[3]

Yet we continue to treat trees as ornaments at best and as commodities at worst. All the while, every one of them gives us the gift of oxygen and stores the carbon we so wildly produce.

The poem "birdbath" is a drama acted by creatures in my own backyard. When the pandemic confined many of us to our homes, I began a vigil from my window. I found solace in the birds and squirrels who nestled and squabbled in the trees. I learned their pecking orders and their feeding times. I heard their mating songs in spring, and noted their quieter nesting periods and the comings and goings of the seasonal visitors. Blue jays are not so common, usually slipping in and out on their way to somewhere. When one settled on the birdbath, and all the others scattered, I admired its beauty, but I also began to worry for the smaller ones. Were their eggs and hatchlings in danger? I have since learned that although blue jays can eat eggs and small birds, they rarely do. They are territorial and will chase other birds away from the areas they claim as their own. Mostly, they feed on seeds and insects. I had "othered" the blue jay without much thought.

3. Simard, *Finding the Mother Tree*, 4.

As I watched, I tried to let the blue jay teach me. After all, the bird village in my backyard doesn't belong to me. I don't get to dictate the behavior of birds. I began to think about how humans are usurpers of land and the gifts it gives; how urbanization, industrialization, and colonialism have dulled our sensibilities to others, human and otherwise, and weakened our ability to learn from them. Can I let the blue jay teach me again about place? About whom is at the top of the food chain and about how much is enough?

The poem "lament for the death of wonder" witnesses the consequences of the dullness that has resulted from our disconnection with creation. We have forgotten how to imagine. We have forgotten how to walk humbly with all creation under the guidance of our Creator. Industrialization has taught us to make idolatries of work and the possession of objects of our own making, without regard for how the making of those objects damages the world around us. We have forgotten our mandate from God to tend and serve what God has made.[4] Some of us have forgotten that a wild world even exists. How can we protect what we have not learned to love?

The poem "say" moves lament into activism. It asks us to stretch our understanding by reimagining the well-known biblical parable of the good Samaritan.[5] Can we extend care to the whole earth, from which we have taken (like bandits) without regard for how our taking has wounded it? In January 2020, this was one of six poems I contributed to an exhibition called "Mother Earth and Her Lovers: Repair and Maintenance" at the MHC Gallery on the campus of Canadian Mennonite University. Through visual art, poetry, and a series of workshops, this exhibition used art to encourage and inspire tired and grieving environmental activists.[6]

These poems are love letters to creation that arise out of my alarm and grief over the losses and changes the climate crisis has created, from extinctions to extreme weather to floods and

4. Gen 2:15.

5. Luke 13.

6. Artists: Bob Haverluck, Rhian Brynjolson, and Sam Baardman.

wildfires. As a person of faith, I am becoming more aware of our mandate from the beginning to tend and keep the earth. I find myself newly attuned to the many places where Scripture gives voice to God's concern for and delight in the more-than-human world.[7] I write, then, to document my growing understanding of my place as just one of God's beloved creatures, to give voice to and advocate for those who don't speak human languages, to celebrate all that is beautiful on this "pale blue dot" in the universe, and to make space for what the more-than-human beings can teach me. I hope my words are also prophetic in the sense of telling the truth about where we are in the story of this world. I hope they bring comfort and dis-ease, encouragement and inspiration.

7. Ps 36:6; Ps 104; Job 38–41.

15

Matthew Owen Gwathmey

Life in the Time of Warming

After David Wallace-Wells

Cascades

A warming planet leads to melting ice,
                which means less sunlight reflected back,
and more soaked up, warming faster still.
                    Means an ocean unable to absorb,
and so greenhouse gases will rise,
                will cause forest and jungle dieback.
Means a hotter climate still, and so on.
                Warmer oceans can take in less heat,
which means more stays in the air,
                which leaves and heats and so on and so on.
A thousand feedback loops cascading,
                the earth pummeled again and again.
The world below our feet, unknown to us.
                None of this is news.

Elements

I.

Deserts expand and the wheat belt moves poleward.
We are hungry. The change coming too fast
for the northern soil to catch up.

II.

Inland flooding, rivers run over, swollen by rain
and storm surges channeled upstream.
The sea level rise draws a new coastline.

III.

The glowing wildfires begin to encroach.
We are canopied by an orange sky.
Where can we go? There's smoke everywhere.

IV.

Prehistoric plagues emerge from the ice.
Ancient diseases return under new names
to home inside us.

V.

The largest lakes have begun to dry up.
Wetlands turn acidic.
Hollowed out, our fantasies of abundance.

VI.

Algae blooms expand the dead zones.
We make these waters unknowable,
the seas and life submerged there.

VII.

Dust exposure and ozone smog
enclosing the planet in a toxic covering.
Blanketed by gray so thick it blots out the sun.

VIII.

The earth will boil with so many disasters,
we'll have to invent new words to describe them.
What roars at us from the ever-worsening fringe?

Kaleidoscope

It's worse than you think. Sound the alarm.
                           Our children, what have we left them?
Dramas to play out in the future,
                     performed by creatures we do not know,
ushered onto the world stage by warming.
                   We are mesmerized by this threat,
living in plastic panic
                      and bee-death parables.
We float, a blip inside a blip.
                   What shape will the next day take?
Calling out into the empty night—
                  momentary, fragile, fleeting.[1]

1. This poem was first written as part of the Choral Creation Lab through the Amadeus Choir in Toronto, Ontario. Parts of it made their way into a longer poem titled "Live Commentary on a Failing Planet" and published in *The Antigonish Review* 216, Spring 2024.

Reflection

"Life in the Time of Warming" is a poem that derives its inspiration from the book *The Uninhabitable Earth* by David Wallace-Wells. Quite simply, you will not be the same after you read this book about the consequences of global warming. We are just starting to see these consequences; we are living in the time of warming. After detailing the current and near-future effects of global warming, Wells does broach the topic of environmental apocalypse in his chapter "Storytelling." He states, "It should be no great prize to be right about the end of the world."[2] Wells then lists various movies, television shows, poems, novels, even a video game, that either directly or indirectly deal with this particular form of the end times. There are a myriad of problems with attempting to tell this story: hero problems, villain problems, as well as the problem of nature and our relationship to it. As Wells argues, "One message of climate change is: you do not live outside the scene but within it, subject to all the same horrors."[3] We are in the story; we are living it. The notion of environmental crisis implies an end game, and we can now hypothesize what this complete and final destruction will look like. Flip to basically any page of *The Uninhabitable Earth* and you will read descriptions of heat, hunger, drowning, wildfire, natural disasters, dying oceans, unbreathable air, plagues . . . you get the idea. The questions must be asked: What value does fictionalizing or narrativizing this very real threat have? Shouldn't we be getting out and doing something?

2. Wallace-Wells, *Uninhabitable Earth*, 104.
3. Wallace-Wells, *Uninhabitable Earth*, 150.

In tracing this view of the end of the world in his book *Ecocriticism*, Greg Garrard goes to, what he considers, the beginning: "The most influential forerunner to the modern environmental apocalypse is the 'Essay on the Principle of Population' (1798) by Thomas Malthus, which set out to contradict the utopian predictions of endless material and moral progress made by political philosopher William Godwin."[4] In this very long essay, two of the arguments that Malthus puts forth are that a continual increase in population cannot be sustained by limited natural resources, and that economic growth does not necessarily mean human growth. Malthus does not describe what this breakdown could potentially look like; however, his prognostication has been used numerous times in order to imagine an environmentally collapsing world. Garrard cites Rachel Carson's *Silent Spring* and Paul Erlich's *The Population Bomb* as two more contemporary examples of environmentalist books that rely "on horrifying apocalyptic projections for [their] persuasive force."[5] These are two popular scientific publications that engage in the fictional practice of imagining a prediction: here are the facts. Here is the evidence. Here is what is happening. Here is what could happen, should we continue down the current path. Much like Wells's *The Uninhabitable Earth*, there is an alarm present in these texts, as well as an inherent call to action.

But what is that call? Back to Garrard, he channels the literary critic Del Ivan Janik, who goes back to D. H. Lawrence and says that he

> saw man as part of an organic universe, living best by acknowledging its wonder and rejecting the temptation to force his will upon it. In this sense he stands at the beginning of the modern post-humanist tradition and of the literature of environmental consciousness.[6]

---

4. Garrard, *Ecocriticism*, 93.
5. Garrard, *Ecocriticism*, 104.
6. Janik, "Environmental Consciousness in Modern Literature," 107.

These ideas are manifested abundantly today, and any text that focuses on ecocritical theory gives several contemporary examples of the importance of ecocentrism, a nature-centered viewpoint, as opposed to anthropocentrism, one that is human-centered. The potential problem arises when this way of thinking is taken to the extreme. It becomes something nihilistic or anti-humanist, with only two possible responses: do nothing, or do harm. It is possible to be ecocentric and humanist. It is of the utmost importance to realize that we exercise this radical empathy for both the human and nonhuman. Garrard concludes his chapter with a somewhat optimistic idea: "Only if we imagine that the planet has a future, after all, are we likely to take responsibility for it."[7]

So here we are in year 2025. The apocalypse is at our door, but the world hasn't ended yet. The titles of the poem's three parts share the same or similar names of the first three parts of Wells's book. "Cascades" brings up the idea of feedback loops. If x happens, then y happens. If y happens, then z happens. If z happens, that makes x worse, which in turn makes y worse, which in turn makes z worse. This process will continue to make the weather more extreme and unpredictable. "Elements" focuses on the effects of climate change across different environments. "Kaleidoscope" is the way we view global warming, watching the changing patterns of rotating colors without fully understanding their significance. The call is to do whatever we can, even write a poem, in order to bring attention to environmental disaster leading to environmental apocalypse and perhaps to affect change. It's not enough, but it is something.

7. Garrard, *Ecocriticism*, 116.

16

Michael Ferber

I Saw You Coming

I saw you coming
before you turned the last bend,
not the professor with the lesson on lateral moraine,
nor the man reading glacial stories in the canyon walls,
but you,
older now,
exuding silence where there had been wonder.

You knew what had happened.
I felt your knowing in the way you stepped,
cautious, like the ground might remember you,
and ache.

You've brought them again,
your students,
though they do not see me yet.
They see ash. They see closure signs.
They see the bare geometry of loss.

But I remember
how you used to speak of me,
my firs feathered in light,
the frost tucked like a secret
beneath the spruce roots,
the V carved by meltwater,
the U a cradle shaped by ice.

You remember, too.
And that is why I have come.

I was cathedral and classroom,
cool breath rising from limestone lungs.
Your students knelt to photograph
lichen, bear scat, the braided streambed,
not knowing how many generations it took
for the moss to climb those north-facing stones.
Not knowing I listened
to each question they asked aloud.

I held the weight of glaciers
before they had names.
The Athabasca ran through my bones
long before your syllabi marked me.

Then came the spark,
embers from up the valley,
carried in wind
too dry for summer.
Fire leapt over the gorge,
and unmade me.

Crown fires tore open my canopy.
The understory curled in on itself.
Birdsong ended in a single night ablaze.
The black spruce sighed
and became silhouette.

There are many to blame, and no one,
but still I burned
and now lie before you naked and afraid of rain.

Now they come,
your students,
and they do not kneel.
They do not climb.
They stay close to the overlook,
as if afraid the valley might take them, too.

But you stay.

And I remember you.

The ash is all you see,
but beneath it,
roots are already listening.
Fireweed presses upward through the cinders.
The mycelium did not die,
it waits,
networked in patience beneath your feet.

Limestone does not mourn
the way a tree does,
but even stone remembers
how to hold a seed.

You will not see forests yet,
but they will come,
in decades, not days.
The valley is not gone.
It is only bare.

And even that is a kind of prayer.

So teach them,
not only how the glaciers and streams carved me,
or why the boreal burns.
Teach them to listen
for the voices that remain.

Tell them
I am still here.

Reflection

Each spring and fall, I take students from my Physical Geography course at The King's University to Jasper National Park in the Rocky Mountains of Alberta. We visit Miette Hot Springs, Pyramid Lake, the Athabasca Glacier, and Maligne Canyon, landscapes where I have taught glacial history, hydrological systems, limestone karst, and ecological succession for nearly two decades. Over the years, the canyon has become more than just a stop on a field trip; it is, for me, a sacred pedagogical place. We descend into it to observe the earth's forms and listen to its long memory of rock layers and water moving beneath our feet. The overlook at Maligne Canyon, where one sees both the sharp hydrological incision of a V-shaped canyon formed by flowing water and the soft contours of a U-shaped glacial-carved valley beyond, has long marked the place where I ask my students to pause and reflect on deep time, landscape change, and the fragile boundaries between human presence and natural process.

In the fall of 2024, we couldn't visit the Canyon. The church where we usually stayed in Jasper had burned in the wildfires that swept through the area that summer, and most of the field trip sites were closed. Instead, I took the class to Banff and Lake Louise. When we returned to Jasper in the spring of 2025 for the three-week intensive version of the course, it was not the canyon that greeted us but the memory of what had been. The trail system was still closed, so we could only visit the overlook. Trees still flanked the path, but only their charred forms. The forest floor was ash, yet the canyon remained. The limestone walls still carried the markings of meltwater, and the river still flowed.

That moment, the return to a place that was both familiar and unrecognizable, inspired the lament that accompanies this reflection. The poem is voiced by the ghost of the living canyon, addressing me as I bring my students back for the first time since the fire. It is not a ghost of malice but of memory. The canyon remembers me. It remembers the previous students who used to kneel to take photos of the lichen below and the spruce trees above. It remembers the canopy that lined the rim and the sound of the wind as it danced across it. But it also remembers the fire, how it tore away the crown and scorched the soil, leaving silence.

The fire that reshaped this part of Jasper began with a lightning strike near Athabasca Falls, several kilometers from the overlook, but it was decades in the making. For years, the forest had held too much dry fuel: standing deadwood left behind by the mountain pine beetle, which has devastated vast swaths of Alberta's boreal forest. Add to this the steady warming of summers and lengthening of dry seasons, and you have a landscape primed to burn.[1] While lightning sparked this particular fire, the ultimate causes are tied to larger patterns of ecological imbalance and climate change. Across the boreal region, fires are becoming more frequent, intense, and expansive. What was once a cycle of renewal is now a pattern of acceleration. As a geographer, I understand these dynamics. But standing at the overlook, seeing what had been lost, I felt something beyond explanation. Science tells us why the fire came. The silence afterward tells us what it took.

In this moment, my role as professor shifts. I do not simply teach about the ecological effects of fire. I bear witness to a landscape that has lost part of itself and yet remains alive. This is the paradox of physical geography. We study systems (glacial, fluvial, atmospheric) that are defined by change, erosion, deposition, and transformation. Even fire is part of the boreal cycle. For thousands of years, fire has played a regenerative role in these landscapes, including through Indigenous burning practices that have sustained ecological balance from time immemorial. But this crown fire feels different. It was not simply part of a recurring rhythm. It was the

1. Gilchrist, "What Our Grief."

product of compounding forces: decades of fire suppression, the erasure of cultural fire stewardship, beetle kill, extreme drought, and a warming climate. My lament, then, is not only for what was lost in this fire but for what seems to be becoming a new normal.

And still, the land endures. Fireweed will come. Aspen roots will send up shoots. The soil, though scarred, still carries memory in its microbial networks. The limestone that anchors the canyon formed over hundreds of millions of years, it has known oceans, ice, and fire before. It is not indifferent, but it is not undone. One of the texts I often use in the course is *Apocalyptic Planet* by Craig Childs.[2] In it, he reminds us that catastrophe and renewal are not opposites in Earth's story. They are companions. The planet has always passed through apocalypse into life again. Reality. Grief. Hope.

This reflection joins others in this volume shaped by visits to Jasper, some written before the fire, others after. In particular, Liana DePoe-Rix's earlier poems, though inscribed at Pyramid Lake, capture times before, when the canyon still offered its full verdant welcome, and after the fire. What I offer here is a different kind of welcome: one marked by absence, but also by resilience. A reminder that even ghosts can speak, and sometimes, they still have something to teach.

2. Childs, *Apocalyptic Planet.*

17

Natalie Crockett

Does Tokitae?

Does Tokitae mourn?
Does she miss her homeland
Where, for four years, she swam by her mother's side?
Does Tokitae recall?
Does she hear screams of young orcas
As they were separated from their mothers' sides, never to return?
Does Tokitae weep?
Does her great eye fill with sorrow
Confused by the new world that she was thrust into—alone?
Does Tokitae know?
Does she remember the open waters
Of the cool, green Salish Sea, as she circles around a tiny tank?
Does Tokitae wish?
Does she long for the quiet of home
As the crowds chant "Lolita," a name not her own?
Does Tokitae see?
Does she take in the blur of faces
Cheering shrilly as she performs year after year without end?
Does Tokitae love?

Does she remember the touch and sound
Of her pod encircling her, providing care now stripped away?
Does Tokitae grieve?
Does she keen for what was lost
Calling for family she has not seen for fifty-one years?

Does Tokitae?

Reflection

On August 8, 1970, Ted Griffiths and Don Goldsberry led a raid on a pod of Southern Resident orcas in the Puget Sound of Washington state. They used speedboats, explosives, and an airplane to force the orcas into Penn Cove.[1] Young orcas were netted to be sold to aquariums, while their distraught mothers swam alongside, crying for their young that would never return. Five orcas were killed during the Penn Cove capture. Their captors slit open the orcas' bellies, filling them with rocks in hopes that the orcas would not be discovered. Their bodies were later found washed ashore.[2]

Tokitae, named after the Chinook word that means "bright day, pretty colors," was one of the young orcas captured from Penn Cove. She was just four years old at the time she was separated from her mother. Tokitae was sold to the Miami Seaquarium, arriving September 23, 1970, where she remained until her death in 2023. The Miami Seaquarium renamed Tokitae "Lolita," a marketable name deemed "more Miami,"[3] and placed her in a pool eighty feet long and twenty feet deep, though wild orcas swim an average of forty miles a day and can dive to depths of five hundred feet.[4] Tokitae herself was twenty-two feet long. Her tank was not given protection from the weather or direct sunlight, and following the death of a companion orca, Hugo, in 1980, she remained alone for the rest of her life.[5] In 2022, Tokitae's performances came to an

1. Orca Network, "Capture."
2. Cowperthwaite, *Blackfish*.
3. Cappiello, "Lolita."
4. Daly, "Orcas Don't Do Well."
5. Orca Network, "Tokitae's Life Now."

end, following public outcry from the release of the film *Blackfish*. One year later, the Miami Seaquarium announced their intent to return Tokitae to an ocean sanctuary in Washington state. These declarations came too late for the orca, who would pass only five months later.[3] Tokitae died in her tank, still calling out the song of the L pod—her family pod–which she remembered fifty-three years after her capture.[6]

I composed this poem in 2021, after learning the history behind Tokitae's capture during a five-week tenure at Whidbey Island where I attended marine biology classes at the environmentally-focused Au Sable Institute. The story was intimately and poignantly recounted to me by Professor Beth Horvath, who had loved and lived beside orcas during a lifetime that extended four times my own. Along with many other Whidbey Island locals, Beth could identify several orcas on the basis of sight, recognizing their markings and family groups. As her voice quavered during the retelling of the event that had occurred fifty years before, I began to think deeply about the plight of Tokitae and other sentient creatures stripped from their homes by human avarice. I use the anaphora "Does" to question the scope of understanding that Tokitae may possess. I recognize the potential folly of anthropomorphizing but simultaneously acknowledge the tension that human-driven change can only come about through human-driven understanding. One does not act until they are moved, and one is not moved if they do not understand. Terms of grief, loneliness, and displacement can reflect individual experiences and invoke this necessary movement. A scientist's first step of knowing is to question, and so I asked "Does Tokitae?" And if so, as I fear she did, may we learn from the atrocities of the past and work towards safeguarding a sustainable future. If we miss the mark by anthropomorphizing the suffering of such creatures as Tokitae, then let us plead guilty to showing greater foresight, greater thoughtfulness, and greater kindness to the inhabitants of our world.

6. deGaris, "Tokitae."

18

Peter Mahaffy

Coupled Souls

ambling along the sun-soaked shore
absorbed in tunes,
unshod sole
ambushed
by crookened thumb of coral
broken, bleached, homeless
lurking angry in the sand
stabs
through calloused human dermal shell
sand stains red
retribution

spasm converges
two worlds
on top and under naked sole

above
a family in the
burbs

nuclear
driven
to the beach
crush of souls seeking
solace in shifting grains of sand

below
teeming underworld of
parents
hermaphrodite
full-moon procreative frenzy
conceives
synchronous snowstorm spawn of eggs and sperm
engaged with current affairs
promise aragonite couplings to grow
millenary family reef

polyps and cousins
secrete skeletons from their closets
suckle riot of bustling marine life
iridescent
harmony of color and sound
fertile festive atoll
feeds the world above the sole

but
burning need for more above
whitewashes flourishing realm below

draglines

cyanide

acidification

eutrophying

blastfishing

trophy diving

warming

two-stroke oil

sunscreen

infections

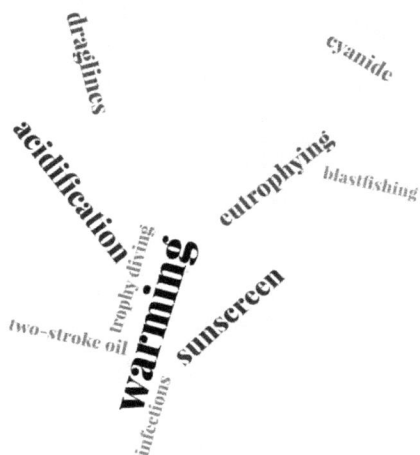

acid-forming air
infiltrates the reef
smothers slap-and-smooth trowels of
carbonate construction crews

blanched with fear
panicked polyps throw algae cells
from crumpling upstairs windows
jagged empty fragments wash ashore
hidden by eddies
await
the saunter of
indifferent soles

can limping bipedal primates
extract earbuds
then deeper wax
tune in the mournful coral dirge
then

lighten imprint in the sand
improvise a living chorus
for coupled souls
above
below
our perforated soles?

Reflection

Living comfortably in the Anthropocene,[1] an epoch of the Geologic Time Scale defined by the heavy imprint of human soles on our planet, we are often unaware that to thrive, we must live in a mutualistic relationship with the ocean coral reefs that nurture a quarter of all marine life and are home to the highest biodiversity on our planet. Yet *homo sapiens* has yet to waken to how the great acceleration of human activity threatens its demise and, ultimately, our own.

One of the major threats to human coastal economies and food security comes from the changing chemistry of the ocean, resulting from powering our planet with fossil fuel combustion. The US National Oceanic and Atmospheric Administration (NOAA) estimates that in 2024, the liquid blue lungs of our planet now dissolve about a third of the CO_2 we send into the atmosphere.[2] While this uptake of CO_2 by oceans slows the rate of atmospheric warming, it has devastating implications for the health of shellfish and corals, whose intricate chemical manufacturing plants rely on the required stable ocean pH and ratio of carbonate to bicarbonate ions to build their skeletons. We lament the cataclysm of careless and willful human activity, including ocean acidification, that rapidly chokes the colors of life from our planet's corals, and we are often oblivious to the whitened and broken signs of destruction that wash ashore. Can we discover the ways in which all creaturely souls above and beneath human feet, on land and in water, and in

1. Crutzen, "Geology of Mankind."

2. National Oceanic and Atmospheric Administration (NOAA), "Ocean Acidification."

the atmosphere and cryosphere, are intricately and dynamically coupled to each other? Can we tune in the funeral dirge of our planet's coral?

Sometimes, feeling the pain of a perforated unshod sole on a sandy beach jolts our souls out of self-absorption.

This lament brings us into the coral reef homes formed by hundreds of thousands of fellow creatures—tiny corals or polyps that nurture and sustain life in marine ecosystems. Living in a mutualistic relationship with the coral polyp animals are photosynthetic algae that in turn make homes in their tissues. The coral protect the algae and give them chemical feedstocks for photosynthesis. The algae return the favor, giving coral back the products of photosynthesis that the polyps turn into proteins, fats, and carbohydrates, and the architectural material need to produce calcium carbonate skeletons.

The scientist-educator inside this poet laments that over half of the world's coral reefs, most of which are far removed from the biggest sources of greenhouse gas emissions, have already been lost or severely damaged by the changing chemistry of the ocean.[3] More than 500 million people around the world[4] rely directly on coral reefs for protection from waves and as barriers to prevent coastal erosion. And coral reefs are the center of activity for a large variety of marine life, as they nurture the many species of fish that coastal populations rely on for food and income.

The grandfather inside this poet laments that grandchildren around the world born this decade may be the last generation to see vibrant, living coral reefs.

The musician inside this poet listens with hope for the faint sounds of a living chorus improvised by coupled creatures on top of and beneath our perforated soles.

3. NOAA, "Over Half World's Coral Reefs."
4. Burke et al., *Reefs at Risk Revisited*, 4.

19

Philip Mingay

The Storm

There is a nagging persistence
That everything is not quite right.
The unpredictable apprehension
Keeps me awake.

The first sign was a canoe
Swirling in the sudden storm.
Then a pine tree, uprooted,
Flew by the window.

It seems consciously malevolent,
Like the poked beast in Pratt's railway poem
Who now has finally had enough.
I stay vigilant.

It can only get worse, I assume.
We are not dissuading its anger.
Other issues take precedence.
I am full of dread.

Reflection

As a youngster, and now as a professor of postcolonial theory and literature, I have always been suspicious of authority and master narratives. My distrust was not necessarily of the truth of narrative but rather the power of words to manipulate, exclude, or deceive. Sitting in church, I wondered why many of the Anglican hymns had militaristic imagery and metaphors. In high school English class, I was fascinated and disturbed by novels such as Joseph Conrad's *Heart of Darkness* and Charlotte Brontë's *Jane Eyre*, and the ruling power's ability to maintain ideological dominance, even while expressing outrage and sympathy about the treatment of the oppressed. Thus, Brueggemann's assertion that "culture has come to accept the claims of empire and a readiness to regard those claims as a given which has its own moral staying power that puts those claims beyond criticism"[1] is particularly troublesome in relation to environmental crisis. Here, the lament as a response to climate change is not dissimilar from postcolonial literary responses in that they both can present as pessimistic and fatalistic, lacking optimism and a future without ideological change. However, that does not mean that they lack humor or hope. Instead, postcolonial literature disrupts master narratives through historical revision and irony.

Within the larger context of postcolonial literature is the unique situation of Canadian literature, with its historical roots in nature. Early Canadian writers were European documenters of the land, focused on its harsh, unforgiving resistance to European settlers, and then spun stories about both its beauty and danger

---

1. Brueggemann, *Reality, Grief, Hope*, 141.

for audiences back home. These nineteenth-century books were wildly successful, with colorful titles such as William Francis Butler's *The Great Lone Land*,[2] M. Davenport's *Journal of a Fourteen Days' Ride Through the Bush from Quebec to Lake Saint John*,[3] or the still popular *Roughing it in the Bush* by Susannah Moodie, who lectures her readers on the last page of her book that

> if these sketches should prove the means of deterring one family from sinking their property, and shipwrecking all their hopes, by going to reside in the backwoods of Canada, I shall consider myself amply repaid for revealing the secrets of the prison-house, and feel that I have not toiled and suffered in the wilderness in vain.[4]

Subsequently, images of nature as a convenient metaphor for Canadian identity were recognized as a persistent theme in Canadian literature. In 1965, literary theorist Northrop termed this nature trope the Garrison Mentality,[5] with the impenetrable and terrifying wilderness forcing Canadians to huddle in garrisons—be they forts, villages, towns, or cities—for physical and psychological safety. In the 1970s, Margaret Atwood, in her book *Survival*, named this imagery the Bush Myth,[6] noting the considerable effect the wilderness had on the fragile Canadian mind, albeit one that reflects a white Canadian settler history, mainly in Ontario.

Yet, despite my academic sensibilities seeing and reading the problematic nature of such theories, often they are hard to discount. In the poem, powerful nature reveals its anthropomorphic spite, and reflects a number of my experiences with nature, ones that quickly turned from ordinary to terrifying. One memory in particular took place on a hot, humid afternoon in the summer of 2018. I was swimming in Muldrew Lake, Ontario, with my family. I could see at the far end of the lake an approaching storm, and

2. Butler, *Great Lone Land*.
3. Davenport, *Journal of a Fourteen Days' Ride*.
4. Moodie, *Roughing It*, 458.
5. Frye, *Bush Garden*.
6. Atwood, *Survival*, 25.

we quickly climbed onto the dock, grabbing towels and water toys and making our way up to the cottage. When the storm hit, much sooner than anticipated, we watched out the windows with a combination of shock and astonishment. It wasn't a tornado—more of a severe windstorm—but it picked up the canoe and tossed it down the shore. In the Canadian shield, the roots of coniferous trees are shallow because of the rocky soil, with some trees stretching their roots across or beneath boulders in search of soil. In the wind, trees collapsed onto the cottage roof, were thrown into the lake, and, in one terrifying sequence, a two hundred-year-old fir toppled parallel into our minivan, driving it into the ground. The next day, arborists had to cut it out in sections so it could be towed. The storm lasted maybe ten minutes, and it became clear that its swath was not that wide, as shortly thereafter, people were on the lake waterskiing, boating, swimming—like nothing had happened. And I suppose for most, it was simply another summer storm, and weather always has the potential to do damage.

But now, whenever I know a storm is approaching, I feel this sense of impending danger, that nature is not to be trusted, and that the storm will always be worse than meteorologists predict. Indeed, it often seems purposely belligerent when it is least expected, a sort of retaliation. Sherrie Malisch believes that such experiences need to be embraced, and that "in an era of climate destabilization, we might do well to open ourselves more fully to the beauty and utility of fear, retreat, limitation, and collectivity, both as literary themes and as real-world practice."[7] This is not to say that we remain gripped in fear, as I was on that day. Instead, we recognize that such encounters expose how "out of step" we are with the natural world.[8]

7. Malisch, "In Praise," 178.
8. Malisch, "In Praise," 186.

20

Ruth Goring

La Niña

"It has never rained so hard in Colombia."[1]
—*THE GUARDIAN*, MAY 10, 2011

In the earth of my skin, in its ashes,
the guitar of me is strummed
for tired songs. Above us, clouds bulge,
balloon, collapse into torrents,
and mountainsides, logged
and grazed to nakedness,
slump into ruin over homes
and paths. Stones lie bewildered,
guava trees plucked like weeds
rot in a tangle of branches.

In the earth of my skin, this lament,
my peasant bones cry *madre mía*,
how we have confounded your calm,
how we have bruised you, our Mother.

1. Delcas, "La Niña," para. 1.

Reflection

I am a poet and artist, not a weather scientist, but I think about climate change every day, whether on my daily walk along Chicago sidewalks leading to Lake Michigan or on my extended visits to the country where I grew up, Colombia.

My poem "La Niña" was written in 2011 and laments the significant impacts of the cooling segment of the ENSO (El Niño Southern Oscillation) cycle that year. In 2021 to 2022, the potential for massive flooding and human displacement in Colombia was again high as I rethought the poem for this book. ENSO itself is a natural cycle that has been documented for centuries—heating (El Niño) followed by cooling (La Niña) of Pacific waters. The problem is that, as with other weather phenomena, climate change is making the related droughts and floods more intense.[2]

Colombia is a stunningly beautiful country, crisscrossed by great and small rivers. The rich land has historically supported countless small family farms. But the effects of climate change— intensified El Niño droughts, La Niña flooding—have added to many decades of rich-against-poor violence that displaced many millions from towns and rural areas. Climate refugees often flee within their own country. The Norwegian Refugee Council, which has worked in Colombia for decades, estimated in 2023 that at least 800,000 Colombians have had to abandon their land because of drought, hurricanes, and other weather events intensified by climate change.[3] In 2024, the country's Constitutional Court ruled

2. Hoyos et al., "Impact of 2010–2011 La Niña."
3. Balasundaram and Tower, "Colombia Moves."

122

that climate refugees must be given the same protections as persons displaced by armed conflict.[4]

More than 80 percent of Colombians now live in cities,[5] while industrial agriculture takes over crop cultivation, applying poisons and stripping forests. I am blessed to know some rural communities that are trying to protect their small-scale farming and mining way of life, but they are few and the economic interests opposing them are vast.

After decades of work in book and magazine editing, I've retired to a tiny condo to focus on writing and making art—and activism, which is another kind of creative work. For example, in 2018, the photographer Michael Bracey and I collaborated on *Caras lindas de Colombia / Beautiful Faces of Colombia*, a bilingual photo book about Afro-Colombian communities.[6] Some of my books are for children; one of these, *Picturing God*, features my own collage illustrations.[7] *Dearworthy: Little Meditations on the Revelations of Julian of Norwich* includes a botanical illustration with each meditation.[8] As for activism, I'm involved in Mennonite Action Chicago, and we carry out beautiful, compelling actions in defense of Gaza, our immigrant neighbors, and others who are targeted by our current authoritarian government. But in a very real sense, all of my creative work is rooted in a Scripture study I was invited to write decades ago.

It was back in 1989 that I embarked on writing *Environmental Stewardship*, which was published later that year by InterVarsity Press.[9] I had already been trying to live lightly on the earth, but now a whole array of Scripture passages celebrating God as the Cosmic Artist dazzled me and won my heart. In Job's poetry, God both mothers and fathers the earth and all its waters—rain, dew, ice, frost (Job 38:25–30). Psalm 104, too, lifts up God's intimacy

---

4. Mendoza, "Colombia."

5. WorldOMeter, "Colombia Demographics."

6. Goring and Bracey, *Caras lindas de Colombia.*

7. Goring, *Picturing God.*

8. Goring, *Dearworthy.*

9. Goring Stewart, *Environmental Stewardship.*

with creatures: God wears light like a garment, gardens the soil so that all have what they need to eat, gives appropriate habitations to storks and mountain goats, renews the ground with the very Spirit of God. Gerard Manley Hopkins's sonnet "God's Grandeur," which I quoted in the study guide, pictures the Spirit brooding over creation "with warm breast and with ah! bright wings."[10]

But passages like Isaiah 5:7–16 and Romans 8:18–27 also told me that the entire creation is abused by evil forces and mourns as it waits for its redemption. I can't detach from this and ignore it. If I love God, I also love what God loves: impoverished Colombian farmers who have become climate refugees and the devastated land itself.

***

Yet, I also can't detach from the earth-destroying system in which I live. I am helplessly complicit. Even though I have donated my car and try to walk and use public transportation as much as possible, many things that I buy and use are transported from afar with fossil fuels. Even though I've become a vegetarian and avoid eggs, my doctor tells me I really need dairy products, which are not exactly clean foods, to maintain my health. (Cattle are among the largest sources of methane emissions around the world, and there are other serious climate effects.[11])

And even though I protest endless war and pray for peace, I pay taxes that help fund the machinery of war—including the gigantic bombs the United States has recently been shipping to Israel so that it can literally burn the life out of the people and land of Gaza, with grave repercussions on the whole earth's air and climate.[12]

All my trips to Colombia have involved air travel. Now that I'm retired, I could travel more slowly by land, but most Latin American buses produce terrible emissions (though there are promising new programs to reduce them).[13] Getting past the

10. Hopkins, "God's Grandeur," line 14.
11. Biology Insights, "Environmental Impact."
12. Lakhani, "Emissions from Israel's War."
13. World Bank, "Green Your Bus Ride."

Darien Gap between Panama and Colombia will involve travel by sea, and boats also burn fossil fuels. And the risk of suffering personal violence will be greater for me as a woman traveling alone in this slow style.

There are solutions, but they require local, regional, national, and international commitments to make radical changes. Such commitments have been much too thin thus far, and as this book goes to press, the Trump administration in the USA is defunding solar and wind initiatives and organic farming supports that Congress and previous administrations had put in place.[14]

***

Can I find a life-path that includes all these imperatives—joy in God's beautiful creation, dogged lifestyle changes to keep shrinking my fossil footprint, anger that fuels resistance (voting, writing letters, protesting, enacting civil disobedience) to our violent systems, and ongoing lament over creation's distress and all that we are losing? How can I keep lament from turning into hopelessness and depression?

The answer—somehow—is love. Earth is our mother and our mother is suffering. Empathy requires that I grieve with her. But love also requires that I keep hoping. I have taken to reminding myself regularly that God, who is Mother of all our mothers, does not abandon what she loves. So I won't either.

I don't really know how to do this, to keep moving forward on this complicated path, holding the grim knowledge of climate change—the grief and angry insistence and hope and love—and stay sane. I think of the Spanish poet Antonio Machado's lines, beloved throughout Colombia and all of Latin America: "Caminante, no hay camino; / se hace camino al andar" (Walker, there is no path; / the way is made by walking).[15] Maybe this, for me and for all who want to be faithful, is what it means to bear our cross to follow Jesus now.

---

14. McDermott, "Trump Administration."
15. Machado, "Proverbios y cantares," sec. 29, p. 106.

21

Sarah Wallace

Bottled Letter

The same thing may be said for all of us, that we do not admire what
we cannot understand.

–MARIANNE MOORE[1]

To Moore, I propose that we also do not admire
what we think is too easily understood: our own
parents, small-town futures, a suite of thirteen
"break-up poems." But to you, I confess,
I don't know how to give myself except as an iceberg,
raising sea levels. I don't know what's clogging
and undulating out there where I have never
traveled. Sometimes, I fear myself to be a man-made
satellite orbiting your gravity, sometimes
a meteor, my trajectory incalculable.

You can unfold the physics of light, refracted
through fish tank, glancing on scales,

1. Moore, "Poetry," 131.

but I become green glass and a dark
speaking. I do not write for truth but for translucence,
or *transulence*—my inadvertent portmanteau of what's
transient and bright and not mine own. The oceans
have become the under-sink where we've tossed our rattling
everything. But this poem keeps bobbing
around like a sealed bottle. It holds forgiveness
for this ooze of love, for what I'll know when I am known.[2]

2. Dillard's *Holy the Firm* informs the tone and theological imagination of
the poem.

Letter from Lake Barnett

for Bruce Buttler, Emeritus Professor of Biology at Burman University

All summer we talk in Zoom gatherings about responsibility
and the Anthropocene: he from his barn-size library,
I from the room that molds me into (almost)
disappearing. In autumn, I return and see Barnett
receding. For four years, I've forgotten to ask him
about the fish bodies I saw bobbing against the bank
one spring day. (I say *bodies* and mean *dead*.)

The surprise of rot in sunlight is better remembered
than all I memorized for his test on geologic time.
So many flashes of silver—the Devonian Age of scaled
change—caught in an inlet. And though that scene sometimes laps
my thoughts more than yesterday's explosion in a distant land,
the reasons for decay might not be even his to offer.
For some, it's heresy to cast the net into the past
or the failing future, the crowded silt and bodies—
fish and (perhaps) God, drowned in the air of our questions.
Holiness holds forth in time, but also death,
mystery, and our (almost) morbid curiosity.

auto-da-fé

At The Anthropocene Project *exhibition*

In Nairobi National Park, they pile ten thousand
tusks—rescued relics of the poachers' trade—and burn
the myth of treasure. The smoke ascends not
forever and ever. These beasts have rest.

Here in the gallery, technology
augments my scraped imagination.
I am there, choked
by smoke and the unassimilable future.

Between the tusks and tonguing flames
there's neither oxygen nor consolation.

Yet, here is a boy, perhaps age two, new
to the delight of legs and wide spaces,
He stumbles and chortles, caught by the crackle
of flame, the release of energy.

Here is the only offering we have left; I cannot name it.

The gallery guard frowns at the mother: "Don't let him touch the
art."

Last Things

After photos of Sudan, the last male northern white rhinoceros,
photographed by Ami Vitale and published in *National Geographic*[3]

He rests on gargantuan knees, skin folding like saints'
robes on marble monuments. His chin sags and wrinkles
like an old man's and his caretaker's hands caress
the jutting head. The man's posture is both benediction
and the fetal curl of pain, the thing that crumbles,
coats your fingers when you reach into the ashes, touch the mar-
tyr's soot.

3. Vitale, "What I Learned."

Reflection

When I write about the Anthropocene, I find myself writing slant, unable to long contemplate the subject by itself. Emily Dickinson combines the injunction "tell all the truth" (line 1) with the acknowledgement that "the Truth must dazzle gradually"[4] because of the "infirm" and childlike capacities of human understanding. With Dickinson, I believe that poetry can sometimes reveal the truth best through an indirect approach to its themes and burdens. Sometimes, environmental writing becomes equated with anodyne nature poetry that obscures the deep enmeshment of humans with what is called "nature," but the realities of anthropogenic climate change and ecological depredation reach—or will reach—into every facet of embodied experience as the widening gyre of the climate crisis increases its victims. Thus, to lament loss and degradation in the natural world is also to lament the changes in which the individual—the lyric speaker or reader—is both implicated and influenced.

My own ecological grief is influenced by my Christian upbringing and my journey from belief in a young earth and an imminent eschaton to an understanding of deep time and present human responsibility. Robert Macfarlane notes that deep time, "the dizzying expanses of Earth history . . . is measured in units that humble the human instant: epochs and aeons [*sic*], instead of minutes and years."[5] In a Christian environment focused on coming apocalypse, I was taught to see Earth as a place of pilgrimage rather than a home. In contrast, to recognize humans as almost

4. Dickinson, "Tell All the Truth."
5. Macfarlane, *Underland*, 15.

incalculably recent parts of Earth's ecosystem makes the story of the earth one that does not begin or end with human life, yet the natural world still opens questions of my own human life within it. This is reflected in the poem "Letter from Lake Barnett," which struggles with the relations of death and beauty and the entwined invitations and limitations of both scientific and existential questions. The Anthropocene may be the arrival of a terrible and unimaginable alterity—"a dark speaking," as the speaker of "Bottled Letter" writes, borrowing from William Tyndale's translation of 1 Cor 13—but it may also be an opportunity to confront what we have thought is "too easily understood," not only "out there" in the other-than-human world but also in ourselves.[6]

I grew up in an environment in which religion was supposed to make everything ultimately understandable and make suffering eventually escapable; this often led to a detachment from the material world's delights and crises. While I have come to more complex—and thus, at times, more troubled—scientific and theological views, religious language and imagery suffuse my writing. Perhaps the language of saints and martyrs memorializes loss and offers a mythology from which to enact resistance and change; perhaps such language is only a bleak relic of sacred myths that failed to uproot greed and exploitation. As a poet, I do not set out to offer definitive answers. I hope readers of these poems can glean a faith that acts for the good of the world in times of seeing darkly, but if even hope and faith fail, may these lamentations also speak attentive love—love for what was, is, and is to come in the beautiful and suffering ecologies we all inhabit.

6. Tyndale, *New Testament*, 1 Cor 13.

22

William Bonfiglio

Pantanal

The orchard is underwater.
The coffee trees have drowned.

Weeds crowd thickly
beneath a surface
clogged with wads
of kariba and hyacinth.
The floating blooms
are deeply violet
in the shadow
of the griseous sky.

A stalk,
a raised neck,
arrows through the sheen of water,
drawing its body forward
with lubricious allure.
It angles toward a thicket,
where strangler figs have encroached

on a stunted grove
of cashew trees.

The seasonal rains carved this plot,
and made a mere
of the clearing.
It rings with a throaty chirping
that rises anonymously
from the fallow.

Something shrieks.
It is not the child
we found fishing off the boardwalk
who continued to scream
Mamões! Mamões aqui!
even after we had shaken our heads
and smiled.

We had thought
the mamões would be plentiful,
that we would be able to reach
and yank them from weighted branches.

The mamões are underwater,
the child no longer there.

Reflection

I have never been to South America. When I drafted the first lines of this piece fifteen years ago, my goal had been to craft a comprehensive, poetic representation of an environment I thought I'd never see. At the time, I was regularly reading travel poetry as an undergraduate studying creative writing at Bucknell University in Lewisburg, Pennsylvania. However, my student financial status prohibited me from making any significant excursions of my own. And as any reader knows, "There is the strange power we have of changing facts by the force of the imagination."[1]

So, I came to know the Pantanal virtually, through travel blogs and YouTube videos and Wikipedia stubs. I paid special care to Indigenous flora and fauna, such as the "kariba and hyacinth," immersing myself in the environment as thoroughly as possible. And as for the narrative of the poem, I speculated how a person might find themselves in the heart of the wetlands, about the kinds of encounters one might have while, say, kayaking with a tour group.

Thus, the poem was, from the start, a tourism piece. And like other tourism pieces—from Rudyard Kipling's "Road to Mandalay"[2] to Jamaica Kincaid's "Colonization in Reverse"[3]—it raises challenging questions regarding agency, spectatorship, and appropriation. The perspective of the tourist is inherently flawed and incomplete, and while some of my observations are fitting given the subject matter—such as allusions to ecological change and environmental trauma—other qualities, such as the use of italics

---

1. Woolf, *Common Reader*, para. 16 under "Montaigne."
2. Kipling, *Collected Poems*, 143–45.
3. Kincaid, *Small Place*, 3–15.

to denote non-English words, seem inappropriate in light of the Pantanal's past and present colonialization. In *Imperial Eyes*, Mary Louise Pratt describes these potentially problematic intersections as "contact zones," places where people and cultures clash.[4]

I wanted to write about the Pantanal because I found it compelling. But I question, today, whether this was my poem to write. I am reminded of the adage often repeated by creative writing instructors to write what you know. I didn't know the Pantanal—not firsthand, anyway. At the same time, I am not trying to assume the voice of an oppressed group.

But I did know anxiety. I know the awful helplessness one feels when considering an environment in decline. I know the sense of removal and impotence, the feeling of being too small and too far to be of any benefit. And I felt I could write about the Pantanal in a way that illustrated this knowledge.

Still, this poem sits uneasily with me today. But despite its flaws, I do like where it ends. To me, it concludes with an unbroachable distance: a deficiency stemming not from loss but from the *inability to have*. Some readers might recognize in this the sublimity of nature, or perhaps the isolated voice of the tourist writer, who will never truly know the space about which they are writing. This deficiency also reflects a challenge inherent to all representative poetry: despite even the poet's best efforts, a piece cannot completely represent its subject; there are simply too many details, too many intangibilities, to include in the poem's limited space.

Thus, "Pantanal" both aspires to representation while acknowledging limits to that aspiration. And while this wasn't necessarily my intention for the poem, it feels an apt juxtaposition.

4. Pratt, *Imperial Eyes*, 91.

Conclusion

Scholar and theologian Walter Brueggemann, who died in 2025, was a transformative voice in the landscape of public theology. His work invited scholars, pastors, poets, and people from all walks of life to see the world more truthfully and to imagine its renewal more boldly. Therefore, the conclusion's structure parallels Brueggemann's prophetic triad of "Reality," "Grief," and "Hope," using our contributor's poems and reflections as examples.[1] Section 1 outlines Reality and the eight ideologies within it. Section 2 details the function of Grief, and Section 3 discusses the possibilities of Hope. Drawing on Brueggemann's insights, our contributors explore poetic realities amid ideologies and systems that have led to ecological degradation and social fragmentation. Each poem and reflection pair is a small act of prophetic imagination,[2] compelling us to pay closer attention to the wounds of creation.

It is important to note that most of our authors are not published poets. Some have never written a poem before. However, they all recognized the opportunity in this book to find a place to imagine creative alternatives to the usual clichéd language applied to environmental predicaments, or to express their positions on topics within their fields without relying on the often sparse, emotionless language of academia. We can discuss poetry in various ways—it describes the indescribable; it provides a space for our emotions—but what is most evident in this book's chapters is our

1. Brueggemann, *Reality, Grief, Hope.*
2. Brueggemann, *Prophetic Imagination.*

need to place the local within the larger context of our everyday work. Rather than limiting an author's voice to a single lens, we aim to illuminate how these poems and reflections collectively reveal the interwoven structures that underlie ecological and social crises. The richness of this volume lies in its overlapping resonances, so readers may see some authors appear under multiple thematic headings.

Section 1: Reality

The book of Lamentations begins with rupture: "How lonely sits the city." Its poetry bears witness to devastation without offering resolution, forcing its readers to dwell in the uncomfortable space in between. For Brueggemann, the prophetic function of lament is to shatter denial, to name reality as it is, and to expose the ideologies that have made ruin possible. Writing in the aftermath of the tragedy of 9/11, Brueggemann challenged illusions of American exceptionalism and entitlement that mirrored ancient Jerusalem. He warned that these narratives, left unexamined, would obscure truth, suppress grief, and foreclose the possibility of hope. In *Climate of Lament*, the poets and authors have undertaken a similar task. They invite us to see more clearly the ideologies that underpin the increasing crises of our day.

The poems and reflections in this volume mourn consequential implications (realities) caused by powerful and persistent ideologies that structure how we relate to creation and one another. This conclusion names and confronts eight such formations. Anthropocentrism and human exceptionalism elevate humanity above the rest of the created world, legitimizing patterns of domination. Shareholder capitalism and economic exploitation reduce life to market value, obscuring justice beneath the veneer of growth. Colonialism, racism, and whiteness function as interlocking systems of dispossession and hierarchy, fragmenting communities and landscapes alike. Technocentrism and the ideology of progress prioritize control and innovation over wisdom and restraint. The ideologies of detachment and disconnection numb our capacity for compassion, while the ideologies of denial and avoidance shield us from uncomfortable truths. Spectatorship fosters a detached, indifferent gaze that transforms suffering into spectacle, allowing us to witness devastation without assuming responsibility or taking action to repair it. And finally, eschatological displacement dislocates hope from the present world, spiritualizing justice into a distant beyond.

1. *Anthropocentrism and Human Exceptionalism*

Anthropomorphism, in its most fundamental form, is the "attribution [usually falsely] of a human form or personality to a god, animal, or thing."[3] On the surface, this allows one to view the natural world from its perspective, potentially leading to empathy and understanding. However, the practice also reveals the "hazy borderlines between human and non-human, can become a powerful tool for questioning the complacency of dominant human self-conceptions."[4] Anthropocentrism, consequently, often coupled with the ideology of human exceptionalism, frames the natural world as subordinate to human life, reducing nonhuman beings to a backdrop or commodity. As Lynn White Jr. argues, such theological frameworks have long authorized the whole of creation as a resource for humans under the guise of responsibility.[5] He traces the roots of environmental destruction to a Christian worldview that interpreted Genesis as a divine mandate for "dominion,"[6] granting humanity license to subdue the earth and its creatures. In contrast, White points toward an alternate position within the Christian tradition: the ethic of stewardship. This vision calls for care, not subjugation, inviting humans to see themselves as responsible members of a larger, living household or *oikos* (the Greek root of "eco" in both "ecology" and "economics"). More recently,

3. *Oxford English Dictionary*, "Anthropomorphism."
4. Clark, *Cambridge Introduction*, 192.
5. White, "Historical Roots," 1203.
6. Gen 1:26–28.

Conclusion

Val Plumwood[7] and Eduardo Kohn[8] have further challenged these hierarchies. Plumwood argues for the decentering of the human within the natural order of species and the cultivation of ecological subjectivity, while Kohn complements this position by calling for an expansion of human identity to include the perspectives and semiotic worlds of nonhumans.

In this anthology, the contributions of Sarah Wallace, Ruth Goring, Cassidhe Hart, and William Bonfiglio directly confront the theology of domination, offering a vision of kinship that dissolves the boundaries between lament for the human and lament for the earth. They draw the reader into what Plumwood might call a more dialogical consciousness, one in which the more-than-human is neither silent nor secondary.[9] Together, these voices offer glimpses of a moral and relational world in which humans are no longer at the center but are one voice among many in a chorus of entangled suffering, resilience, and beauty. In contrast to human exceptionalism, both Indigenous and Christian traditions offer alternative frameworks rooted in relationship rather than dominance. Robin Wall Kimmerer, in *Braiding Sweetgrass*, draws from her Potawatomi heritage to reveal the world as a "web of reciprocity."[10] Creation, in this view, is animated by mutual care, and the harm we cause emerges from a failure to remember our place within that relational web. The first command to humanity in Gen 2:15 offers a stewardship model grounded in responsibility and restraint. Lament, as it unfolds across the poems in this volume, becomes a necessary act of ideological unlearning by opening space for reimagining our place in creation.

7. Plumwood, *Environmental Culture*.
8. Kohn, *How Forests Think*.
9. Plumwood, *Environmental Culture*.
10. Kimmerer, *Braiding Sweetgrass*, 307.

2. *Shareholder Capitalism*

Today's form of capitalism, marked by shareholder prima-
cy, market fundamentalism, a fixation on GDP growth, and
extractive economic logic, has normalized the exploitation of
both people and planet. It commodifies land, labor, and life,
reducing ecosystems to extractive zones and workers to cost
centers. As Andrew Hoffman reminds us, this version of capitalism has achieved immense material gains for a privileged
few at a profound ecological and social cost.[11] Rather than a
natural law, this form of capitalism is a cultural and political
construct, one that can and must be reshaped. The current
form has treated nature as both a limitless resource and an
endless landfill, while concentrating wealth in the hands of
the few. Yet, capitalism need not be governed by exploitation.
As Hoffman and others have argued, the market is a human
institution that can be reoriented toward reciprocity, mutual
benefit, and shared flourishing.

The works of Jeremiah Bašurić, Connie Braun, Sarah
Wallace, and Joanne Moyer bring this ideological critique
to life by embodying the consequences of extractive logic in
personal, ecological, and theological forms. Bašurić's narrative, in particular, unfolds along streets lined with boarded-
up storefronts and broken promises, revealing the violence of
disinvestment and the myth of trickle-down economic hope.
Collectively, these contributions expose the myths that prop
up capitalism's current form: the illusion of endless resources
for growth, the sanctity of profit, and the denial of interdependence. They call us to reimagine the market not as a zero-sum
arena of competition, but as a space of mutual flourishing.
In *Materiality as Resistance*, Brueggemann discusses how we
can choose to continue propagating degradation through
exploitation by inhabiting roles such as user, consumer, pos-
sessor, exploiter, or predator. He contrasts these by unpack-
ing alternatives such as heir, neighbor, partner, and citizen.[12]

11. Hoffman, *Business School*, 21.
12. Brueggemann, *Materiality as Resistance*, 82–84.

3. *Colonialism, Racism, and Whiteness*

Colonialism has redrawn borders, dispossessed Indigenous peoples, and reshaped our relationships with land, memory, and one another. Researchers Eve Tuck and K. Wayne Yang insist on material reparations and the dismantling of settler systems that persist in environmental and cultural devastation.[13] In their framework, "whiteness" operates not simply as a personal identity but as a structure that privileges erasure and distance from consequence. Such ideological formations continue to shape contemporary environmental injustice, as geographer Laura Pulido has argued, not merely through individual privilege but through systemic white supremacy embedded in how cities are built, resources extracted, and people abandoned by social and economic systems.[14]

In *Climate of Lament*, Jane Satterfield's work exposes how settler myths are entrenched in domestic and maternal spheres, suggesting that coloniality seeps into our most intimate spaces. Likewise, Lori Matties explores the layered inheritances of Mennonite complicity with colonialism, narrating how land, theology, and silence intersect in patterns of forgetting and moral convenience. William Bonfiglio confronts whiteness directly, naming its evasions, confessions, and spiritual failures. In doing so, he echoes the call of theologian Willie James Jennings, who argues that Christianity must reckon with its racialized imagination if it is to offer any viable vision of repair.[15] Jeremiah Bašurić explicitly names whiteness as an operating system that had a profound effect on his childhood. His lament emerges from the silence and denial that whiteness demands from those who are othered. Together, these contributors unmask the colonial and racial foundations of environmental harm.

13. Tuck and Yang, "Decolonization Is Not a Metaphor."
14. Pulido, "Geographies of Race and Ethnicity."
15. Jennings, *Christian Imagination*, 6.

4. *Technocentrism and Ideologies of Progress*

Among the most pervasive idols lamented in this volume is "progress," the belief that technology, scientific innovation, and economic growth will inevitably lead us to salvation. This ideology insists that mastery over nature is not only possible but virtuous, framing ecological limits as problems to be overcome rather than realities to be respected. In their book *The Transforming Vision*, Brian Walsh and J. Richard Middleton warn that modern Western culture, while appearing to reject divine authority, continues to worship an "unholy trinity" of scientism, technicism, and economism.[16] In *Climate of Lament*, Ashley Sakundiak mourns the disintegration of such sacred relationships under the weight of technological abstraction, and suggests that lament is not a rejection of human achievement but a call to recover humility, memory, and care. Similarly, David Rutherford critiques the unchecked expansion of human-centered development, urging instead a recognition of finitude and ecological interdependence. Thus, these poets resist the assumption that technological innovation alone can solve what is fundamentally spiritual and relational.

5. *Detachment and Disconnection*

Detachment is a condition in which we come to experience nature, others, and even ourselves as disposable and disconnected.[17] In such a state, land becomes a mere resource, and neighbor is transformed into competitor.[18] Martin Buber warned of this fragmentation long ago, describing the shift from *I–Thou* relationships, which are characterized by intimacy and reciprocity, to *I–It* relationships, which instrumentalize and objectify.[19] This epistemic and emotional distance not only erodes our moral imagination but also enables the very systems of exploitation and denial lamented in this volume.

---

16. Walsh and Middleton, *Transforming Vision*, 132.

17. Berry, *Dream of the Earth*, 2.

18. Berry, *Unsettling of America*, esp. 4–7.

19. Buber, *I and Thou*.

Cynthia Wallace's reflection mourns the disorientation wrought by theological estrangement, naming the way disembodied faith can reinforce ecological neglect through "legal decrees." In tracing a return to embodied prayer and place-based presence, she urges a reintegration of spirituality and soil, despite the "smoke stinging her eyes."[20] Lamenting the psychological and communal costs of modern agriculture and environmental apathy, Justin Mullikin draws our attention to the effects of colonial indifference on important issues, such as indigenous crops. Therefore, the lament of disconnection serves as a first step toward communion and reconnection. The grief here is for the rupture of belonging (the tearing apart of land, people, and culture) that Wendell Berry warns against.[21] Readers are invited to move from isolation to connection through genuine, embodied relationships with one another, the land, and the sacred.

6. *Denial and Avoidance*

If the dominant ideologies of our age are fueled by exploitation and disconnection, they are sustained by a subtler force: the refusal to see. Denial and avoidance function as the moral adhesive that binds these systems together, permitting us to acknowledge devastation at a distance. As Stanley Cohen has shown in *States of Denial*,[22] this is not a matter of ignorance but of "knowing and not knowing," a collective mental choreography that includes interpretive ("It's not as bad as it seems"), implicatory ("I know it's true, but I can't act"), and emotional ("If I allow myself to feel this, it will destroy me") forms of denial.[23] Lament arrests the impulse to look away.

Several works in this volume resist the ideological pull toward numbness and distraction. For example, Natalie

---

20. p. 34.

21. Berry, *Life Is a Miracle*.

22. Cohen, *States of Denial*.

23. Cohen, *States of Denial*, 1–19.

Crockett's emotional poem calls readers to face not only the suffering of the earth but also our complicity in its silencing. And Francesca Tronetti's contribution uncovers corporations functioning as citizens, pretending to be part of communities when they are actually harming them, especially those marginalized by race or class. Ched Myers names the "myth of innocence," reminding us that denial is an active refusal to see, a deliberate stance that preserves privilege by shifting blame to those actually deserving of empathy.[24] The laments gathered here expose this myth and signal a different possibility. By drawing us into emotional and moral proximity with loss, these works rupture the denial that has allowed it to persist. In doing so, they offer us the courage to expose what is happening in our own communities and landscapes.

7. *Spectatorship*

We admit that the term "spectatorship" sounds like it wandered in from a graduate seminar. Nonetheless, it belongs in this collection because it names something deeply familiar and spiritually perilous: the tendency to watch suffering without being moved to act. It is shaped by the long shadows of empire, where the powerful have learned to view colonized peoples and lands from afar, through the distorting lens of superiority and control. In modern contexts, this gaze is perpetuated through media, technology, and even some forms of education, where environmental destruction and human displacement are encountered as distant media content rather than urgent, shared crises. It is no secret, for example, that smart phone use causes "'absence presence:' [the] condition of being physically present but mentally and emotionally absent [that] undercuts the quality of interpersonal interactions that produce social connection."[25] As Susan Sontag writes, when we constantly view images of suffering (war, disaster, ecological ruin), we can begin to treat them as visual

---

24. Myers, *Binding the Strong Man*, 10.
25. Leister, "When Cell Phones Replace People," para. 6.

objects to be consumed in feigned outrage rather than calls to specific moral response. Instead of prompting compassion or action, these images risk dulling our empathy.[26] This spectatorship perpetuates systems of harm by allowing those with privilege to observe without intervening.

Jane Satterfield's poems highlight how empire is not only historical but ongoing, often encoded in how we frame and consume others' stories. Drawing from the visual language of protest and presence, her poetry recalls Ariella Azoulay's call for a civic contract between viewer and subject—one in which looking must lead to responsibility.[27] Ruth Goring, too, refuses passive mourning. Her writing places the reader amid rupture, inescapably located in what Edward Said might call the "textual field of imperialism," where how we see is shaped by where we stand.[28] Matthew Gwathmey's criticism that "none of this is news" reinforces that in spectatorship, headlines about environmental degradations never cease, yet fail to prompt us to action. These works disrupt the illusion that we can be innocent bystanders, insisting instead on an ethic of entanglement and embodied witness. With our social media saturated with images of catastrophe, lament invites a different gaze that is active and reciprocal, rather than the imperial gaze that represents nature (and people) as inferior and in need of mastery.

8. *Eschatological Displacement*

This ideology embodies a deferral of responsibility by pessimistically seeing hope, healing, and justice as unattainable, distant horizons, or as inevitable consequences of our consumptive system. Instead of confronting the damage done to land and neighbor and seeking renewal and restoration, eschatological displacement reorients longing away from earthly restoration and toward heavenly escape.

26. Sontag, *Regarding the Pain of Others*, 70–75.
27. Azoulay, *Civil Contract of Photography*, 20–23.
28. Said, *Orientalism*, 7–12.

Brueggemann might describe seeking such an escape or place as "u-topian ('no place'),"[29] in contrast to "participation in, attentiveness to, and loyalty to a place."[30] It numbs moral imagination and disables faithful action.

In this volume, Edudzinam Aklamanu's vivid memory of the 2016 Fort McMurray, Alberta, wildfire evokes the language of apocalypse and points toward *parousia*—the second coming—while also underscoring the urgency of earthly care. Both Lori Matties and Cynthia Wallace challenge traditions that spiritualize, and consequently legitimize, ecological destruction. Alice Major and Justin Mullikin also disrupt the assumption that the earth is merely a temporary vessel to be discarded. Insightfully, Major's attention to the nuances of noise in our lives exposes the fragility of place, but at the same time reveals how resilient nature can be, and how quickly it "returns" to its inherent state once human intervention disappears.

Thus, the volume's lamentations call us to reframe eschatology not as displacement but as engagement. The longing for renewal, so central to apocalyptic literature, need not abandon the earth. Instead, it can become a source of moral courage for its healing. Theologically, this means reclaiming visions like Isaiah's peaceful kingdom or Revelation's new Jerusalem as stimuli to cultivate justice, tenderness, and ecological integrity in the present.

Section 2: Grief

Grief, as Brueggemann reminds us, is the bridge that leads from a truthful reckoning with reality toward the possibility of hope. Having used the breadth of laments in this volume to name the destructive ideologies that sustain ecological devastation and social fragmentation, we turn now to how lament can be a viable

29. Brueggemann, *Materiality as Resistance*, 78.
30. Brueggemann, *Materiality as Resistance*, 80.

option for our grief. Our contributors offer laments that beckon us to inhabit grief as a necessary passage, one that invites both personal transformation and the reimagining of shared life. In this section, we will draw upon individual poems with greater attentiveness to reveal the shared resonances that call us toward communal renewal.

Lament begins in the body, in the intimate ache of loss as it is felt somatically. The personal griefs shared in this volume are lived experiences of disorientation in the face of ecological collapse and social harm, be it a scorched forest or vanishing green spaces. Ashley Sakundiak's "Lifeless" roots lament in the scarcity of water that scarred her family's pasture, a place bound to her identity and memory. Watching the land fail those it once sustained, Sakundiak names the grief of witnessing the erosion of a place that has nurtured belonging. David Rutherford's "A Place Transformed" traces the loss of place through urbanization and the erasure of local character. Rutherford's writing gives voice to solastalgia,[31] the homesickness one feels while still at home, as place is hollowed out and commodified. His lament teaches that personal grief is inextricably linked to the larger forces that shape landscapes and lives.

Further, Liana DePoe-Rix's suite of poems explores grief at the intersection of ecological loss, personal trauma, and the struggle for resilience. In "Small," "hazy clarity," and "On Pyramid Lake (from Afar)," DePoe-Rix names the ache of helplessness in the face of overwhelming loss, both personal and planetary. Her lament also reveals the particular weight borne by young adults in a time shaped by overlapping crises, as personal loss and trauma unfolding alongside the emerging awareness of ecological collapse and social fracture.

These laments remind us that ecological grief is never merely about nature and the external world; it is always also about our internal world: the places that have shaped us, the relationships that tether us, and the identities formed in and through place. Human Geographer Yi-Fu Tuan refers to this as "topophilia," a profound emotional connection to place that binds memory, meaning, and

31. Abram, *Spell of the Sensuous.*

identity to the landscapes we inhabit.[32] To grieve personally is to honor these bonds, to refuse the numbing logic of avoidance, and to begin the difficult, necessary work of seeing what has been lost.

However, if personal lament gives voice to the intimate experience of loss, collective lament draws us into shared mourning, binding individuals into community through the act of naming grief together. Communal laments remind us that ecological devastation is not suffered alone. They create a space in which grief can be held, shared, and honored before responsibility is assigned and before solutions are sought. Joanne Moyer's liturgical lament offers one such communal voice. Drawing on Scripture, the structure of liturgy, and the framework of Planetary Boundaries, Moyer gives form and language for communities to grieve together: the lost bison, the poisoned monarch, the choking smoke, the bleaching reefs. Each refrain, "The earth mourns. We mourn with it. Lord, have mercy," becomes a collective breath, allowing the gathered body to dwell in sorrow without immediately seeking to justify or fix the problem. Similarly, Michael Ferber's lament, voiced through the ghost of Maligne Canyon, is also a meditation on communal grief. By personifying the canyon as a living interlocutor, Ferber frames grief as a communal response to the fragility of place. Yet even amid charred landscapes, the poem hints at renewal through fireweed pushing through ash and the unseen work of roots and mycelium, reminding readers that communal lament is both an expression of loss and a seedbed for hope.

Intersectional grief is the layered sorrow that arises when ecological, social, and historical losses intersect. Rather than treating environmental mourning as separate from human histories, it recognizes that the destruction of ecosystems and species is entangled with the isms and ideologies above, systems of colonialism, racial violence, capitalist extraction, and industrialization. As Ashlee Cunsolo and Neville Ellis argue, ecological grief is both an emotional and political response to the loss of ecosystems, species,

---

32. Tuan, *Topophilia*.

and meaningful landscapes that are often tied to broader histories of exploitation and injustice.[33]

Jane Satterfield's poetry embodies this intersectional grief by refusing to separate ecological loss from the histories of violence and exploitation that underpin it. For example, in "Endling," an elegy for the last male northern white rhinoceros, she laments the death of a species and identifies the entangled forces of colonial trade, poaching, and capitalist desire that have driven it to extinction. Likewise, Lori Matties's laments trace the intersections of ecological devastation, colonial histories, and spiritual complicity, mourning not only the losses themselves but the systems that have made them inevitable. In "fall," the death of Winnipeg's urban forest becomes an emblem of human shortsightedness: monocropped trees, planted for aesthetics, now marked for removal under the city's orange dots of death. And Connie Braun's poetry inhabits what she calls the "house of mourning," a space where personal, historical, and ecological grief converge. As a child of postwar refugee immigrants, Braun writes from the layered memory of displacement and trauma, linking her family's history of survival with present-day crises of climate change, migration, and systemic violence

How is loss experienced at an intimate level, while also stretching across the vastness of climate systems, extinction events, and intergenerational futures? Experiencing grief at multiple scales can be disorienting and incomprehensible, as if the human heart cannot contain the enormity of what is being lost. As Michael Ferber and Randy Haluza-DeLay argue, scale-jumping, the ability to move between local experiences and planetary narratives, reveals both the challenge and necessity of moral imagination, allowing us to see how a single burned forest, a vanished species, or a polluted river is bound to the larger story of a planet in crisis.[34] Scholars such as Ashlee Cunsolo[35] and Glenn Albrecht[36] describe this plan-

33. Cunsolo and Ellis, "Ecological Grief," 275–81.

34. Ferber and Haluza-DeLay, "Scale-Jumping and Climate Change," 193–210.

35. Cunsolo and Landman, *Mourning Nature*, 45.

36. Albrecht, *Earth Emotions*.

etary grief as a response to "slow violence," the incremental, often invisible harm of environmental change. Lament across scales, then, is both a spiritual and imaginative act: it binds the local to the global.

Francesca Tronetti's lament in this collection begins at the intimate scale of family and body, with skin blistered, wombs poisoned, and livelihoods destroyed, yet her reflection reveals how this grief is both local and planetary: it describes villages abandoned in Western Pennsylvania or Hinkley, California, but also echoes in every place where short-term gain has left enduring scars on land and lives. Continuing this theme, Peter Mahaffy's lament for the coral reefs mourns not only their loss but our diminishment. Driven by climate change, particularly ocean acidification caused by carbon emissions, these reefs now bleach, fracture, and wash ashore, their "carbonate construction crews" halted by a changing ocean chemistry. Yet in grief, Mahaffy listens for possibility: might the pain of contact, of feeling the reef's fragments beneath us, wake us from disconnection? Philip Mingay's "The Storm" captures the unsettling unpredictability of a world where human and natural forces collide. His vivid account of uprooted pines, windlashed canoes, and the ominous sense that "everything is not quite right" connects the personal fear of a single storm to the larger reality of climate destabilization. In his reflection, Mingay draws on postcolonial critiques of master narratives to expose how we often frame nature as either a passive backdrop or a hostile force to be subdued, a framing that has historically masked ecological harm.

Section 3: Hope

In this final section, we see how hope is a way of living into brokenness with imagination, care, and persistence. The laments gathered here have named the harm and held us in the weight of grief, but they have also traced the contours of what could be restored. Hope emerges where we dare to reimagine all our relations. *Laudato Si'*, Pope Francis's encyclical on care for our common home, reminds us that ecological and social crises are inseparable, both rooted in a broken sense of kinship and mutual responsibility. He calls for an "integral ecology," one that recognizes the earth not as an object to exploit but as a living community to which we belong.[37] This vision of interdependence resonates throughout the laments in this volume, where grief over environmental destruction is also grief for the fractures in our collective life.

Cassidhe Hart's "A Lament According to Psalm 22" and subsequent reflection reimagine the ancient cry of abandonment as the voice of a crucified Earth, groaning under the weight of exploitation and neglect. Like the psalm it mirrors, Hart's poem moves from desolation to a vision of restoration, one in which creation's voice is rejoined with the Creator's, and the fractured web of life is remembered and renewed. Further, Jeremiah Bašurić's "Tanaga Lament" calls us to reimagine hope as a theological and relational reclamation. Drawing from the Filipino tanaga form and informed by Willie Jennings's critique of whiteness as a diseased theological imagination,[38] Bašurić laments the ways in which Christianity has been co-opted by systems of control that sever land, body, and spirit from their sacred interdependence. Bašurić's reflection, then, underscores that hope does not arise from forgetting the wounds of history but from confronting them, naming the ways that faith has been distorted, and returning to a vision where land and community are "living organizers of identity." Also, Natalie Crockett's "Does Tokitae?" begins in lament but gestures toward a hope forged through empathy and moral awakening. Her poem's insistent questions, "Does Tokitae mourn? Does she recall? Does she grieve?" refuse to allow the orca's suffering to remain an abstraction or a distant spectacle. In this way, Crockett's lament joins the chorus of the volume, transforming personal sorrow for a single orca into a shared vision for restoration and the dignity of all creation.

Alice Major's "City Birds Sing Louder" reminds us that hope can emerge not only from large-scale action but from the quiet clarity that follows disruption. In her poem, the sudden hush of

37. Francis, *Laudato Si'*.
38. Jennings, *Christian Imagination*.

pandemic lockdowns becomes a rare gift, allowing the hidden sounds of the world, especially birdsong, to break through the constant industrial din. Her work suggests that hope does not always arrive in grand gestures but in the humble recognition that renewal begins with the space we create for other voices to be heard, whether they belong to sparrows, rivers, or the earth itself. Finally, Justin Mullikin's "Pantanal" traces the quiet dignity of coffee trees half-submerged and hyacinths drifting like violet prayers, a vision both haunted and alive. In his reflection, Mullikin wrestles with the distance between observer and subject, acknowledging the discomfort of bearing witness without easy resolution. Yet this unease becomes a kind of reverence, a recognition that hope begins when we choose to look closely and humbly at the places where life struggles to endure.

Conclusion

Brueggemann wonderfully describes how "what emerges on the lips of the poet is a new world now being given and now being received."[39] Lament, as the contributors to this volume have shown, is not an end but a necessary beginning. It names the fractures we would rather ignore and compels us to stand within them long enough to see clearly. Through lament, we learn to speak truth against the ideologies that have diminished both people and planet, to face the pain that myths of progress would erase, and to listen to the human and more-than-human voices that carry stories of both wound and resilience. Grief has taught us to feel loss and to name its weight without turning away, as in the time of Lamentations. "The generation of Israelites who lived through and looked back on the destruction of Jerusalem drew very close to despair. How could they not! The destruction of the city and the deportation of the king visibly negated all of the certitudes upon which they had counted."[40] Yet, as then, hope now emerges as the creative and

---

39. Brueggemann, *Reality, Grief, Hope*, 128.
40. Brueggemann, *Reality, Grief, Hope*, 90.

communal work of reimagining what might yet be made whole. It is found in the renewed kinship of reimagined relationships, in the acts of solidarity that bind neighbors and strangers into shared responsibility, and in the attentive presence that sees beauty even in scarred landscapes. Hope is not a quick escape from pain; it is the determination to live with open eyes, to honor what has been broken, and to begin again with care and reverence.

The poems and reflections gathered here offer both testimony and invitation to the importance of place. They call us to practices that sustain hope: to plant trees in burned soil, to tell the stories of the places and creatures that have shaped us, and to walk with humility toward repair. Hope is participatory, not passive; it is born in small and stubborn gestures. Each of us must abandon our utopia ("no place!") and find our literal places on the planet to begin these acts. Brueggemann shared that "everyone comes from somewhere. Everyone comes from a particular place with its particular hope and particular resources and particular social protocols and particular foods . . . we must be obligated, contributing partners in a time and place."[41] May this volume inspire you to move from the grief of places lost or ruined to be "a contributor to creaturely well-being" in the places you love.[42]

41. Brueggemann, *Materiality as Resistance*, 81.

42. Brueggemann, *Materiality as Resistance*, 12.

Contributor Biographies

Editors/Contributors

Michael Ferber

Michael P. Ferber (PhD, MBA, MDiv, MEd) is the dean of the Leder School of Business at The King's University in Edmonton, Alberta, where he teaches courses in business, environmental studies, and geography. His scholarship and writing explore the intersections of social, environmental, and economic sustainability, drawing on his background in human geography, among other disciplines. Michael has published essays on topics ranging from the geography of religion to education to international development. He is active in the nonprofit sector, serving as board chair of e4c, a social service organization in Edmonton, and as a board member of World Vision Canada. Additionally, he is a long-standing instructor with the Au Sable Institute for Environmental Studies. Originally from West Virginia, he brings together southern storytelling and Canadian perspectives in his work, seeking to integrate faith, justice, and care for creation.

Philip Mingay

Philip Mingay is an associate professor of English at The King's University in Edmonton, Alberta, Canada, where he teaches post-colonial and Canadian literature, literary theory, and film. His main interest is the relationship between visual arts and literature, particularly the representation of painters and how the stereotype of the asocial European artist has translated historically to early colonial literature. Philip has been teaching undergraduate students for more than half his life and still enjoys inviting them to see the power and wonder of literature and poetry. He has also written about pedagogy and introductory courses, and art education in early Canadian literature.

Contributors

William Bonfiglio

William Bonfiglio's poetry has been awarded a Pearl Hogrefe Grant in Creative Writing Recognition Award, the Julia Fonville Smithson Memorial Prize, and has appeared in *Gulf Coast, Salt Hill Journal, New Letters*, and elsewhere. He lives on the unceded, unsurrendered territories of the Wolastoqey, Mi'gmaw, and Peskotomuhkati peoples.

Connie Braun

Connie T. Braun (MA Humanities, MFA) is an author of nonfiction, a poet, instructor of creative writing, and has involvements and interests that span arts, education, social justice, and peace, and more recently, bee keeping and a small vineyard—pursuits that seem a perfect blend. Her essays and poetry appear in literary and academic journals: among them, *Ekstasis, Equinox, Journal of Religious Studies and Theology, Notre Dame Review, Prism International, Room Magazine, Renaissance: Essays on Values in Literature*, and *Consequence*, where she has recently joined the editorial committee. Her poetry has been anthologized in North America and internationally, including in *Blue will Rise Over Yellow: An International Anthology for Ukraine*; *Scars* (Berlin, Germany); *Drawing Near: Devotional of Art, Poetry and Reflection* (US); and *ConVersing ConServing Ecopoetics* (Fern Hill Publications); *In/ Words Magazine Special Issue: "Refuge(e)"* (Carleton University);

Force Field 77 BC Women Poets; and *150+ Canada's History in Poetry*. She is the author of the memoir *The Steppes are the Colour of Sepia* (Ronsdale) and the essay collection *Silentium: And Other Reflections on Memory, Sorrow, Place, and The Sacred* (Resource Publications). Her latest book is *Moonroads: Poetry* (CMU Press, Winnipeg, 2025). Connie makes her home in British Columbia, Canada.

Jeremiah Bašurić

Jeremiah Bašurić is a co-senior leader of intercultural ministry of the Christian Reformed Church in Canada and a pastor at mosaicHouse Church, a multicultural Christian Reformed Church plant in Edmonton, Alberta. He is also hospital chaplain and a volunteer inner-city chaplain. From his Croatian father, he has developed a love for soccer. From his Filipino mother, he has developed a love for singing. When he is not eating Filipino food or playing music, you can find him hiking in the mountains with his Canadian-Dutch-Frisian wife, Sarah, who is a registered nurse. She is studying to be a counselor to support first responders experiencing trauma.

Natalie Crockett

Natalie Crockett grew up in the heart of Tennessee, USA, spending her summers rescuing crawdads and tadpoles from dry creek beds and carrying them to deeper waters. Her passion continued through her undergraduate degree, as she worked on conservation of the hellbender salamander and spent her free time collecting jumping spiders for research studies. She secured a BS in biological sciences, along with a minor in English, from Lee University in 2023. Natalie can now be found in Florida, where she lives exactly eleven minutes from the beach and often spends an enjoyable evening watching dolphins in the gulf.

Liana DePoe-Rix

Li DePoe-Rix (they/them) has always been fascinated with the natural world around them. From bird-watching to hiking, nature continues to be a source of joy, inspiration, and well-being. They do their best to support their community, be it through activism, like starting a Gay-Straight Alliance at their Christian school, or just through being a friend to those in need. They have always found solace in art, poetry, and music, and hope to one day create and publish novels and poetry collections.

Ruth Goring

Ruth Goring writes, makes art, prays, and does political organizing in Chicago, Illinois, USA. In 2024, she published *Dearworthy: Little Meditations on the Revelations of Julian of Norwich* (Anamchara Books) with her own botanical illustrations. Her third poetry collection is *The Authority of Hunger* (Fernwood, forthcoming); earlier collections are *Soap Is Political* (Glass Lyre, 2015) and *Yellow Doors* (WordFarm, 2003). She has also published books for children: *Isaiah and the Worry Pack* (IVP Kids, 2021); *Picturing God* (Beaming Books, 2019); and *Adriana's Angels* (Sparkhouse Family, 2017; also in Spanish as *Los ángeles de Adriana*). Ruth translated Marlena Proper Graves's *The Way Up Is Down* [Para subir hay que bajar] into Spanish (IVP Español, 2024) and Aurora Posada de Gregorio's *Sin remitente* [No Return Address] into English (Fig Factor Media, 2023). Ruth is involved in a lively multicultural Mennonite congregation in her neighborhood, Living Water Community Church, and acts politically with Mennonite Action Chicago. She cherishes closeness to her siblings, children, and grandchildren, and outside her little condo, she tends a flourishing little garden of native plants. Find her at ruthgoringbooks.com.

Matthew Owen Gwathmey

Matthew Gwathmey lives in Fredericton, New Brunswick, on Wolastoqey Territory with his partner, Lily, and their five children. He has published three poetry collections: *Our Latest in Folktales* (Brick Books, 2019); *Tumbling for Amateurs* (Coach House Books, 2023); and *Family Band* (The Porcupine's Quill, 2024). His fourth collection is forthcoming in 2027 with Brick Books.

Cassidhe Hart

As a poet and liturgist, Cassidhe Hart writes at the intersection of faith, ecology, community, and ritual to explore the ways we tell stories about our inner and outer worlds. She received her master's degree of divinity from Garrett-Evangelical Theological Seminary and is a member of Reba Place Church, a congregation within the Mennonite Church USA, located on the ancestral land of the Council of Three Fires in Evanston, Illinois. Because she comes from a long line of white settler-colonists, Cassidhe is committed to centering systematically oppressed voices and to growing an anti-racist, decolonizing ethic in all her work. She has been commissioned to write prayers, liturgies, and songs for worship services, retreats, workshops, podcasts, and other settings with a contemplative and ecological focus. Learn more about her writing and ways to connect at cassidhehart.wordpress.com.

Edudzinam Aklamanu

Edudzinam Aklamanu was born on a warm, rainy day in June in Ghana to Sachiel and Vernicia Aklamanu. In 2015, Edu moved with four siblings and parents to Fort McMurray, Canada, experiencing a dramatic shift from +34 °C to –30 °C. Clutching a not-so-warm winter jacket while making her way to the car, Edu second-guessed the decision to move but now calls Canada home. Edu attended Westwood Community High School before pursuing studies in biology and kinesiology at The King's University, where participation in *Climate of Lament* was encouraged. With a love for giving back and engaging with the community, Edu also serves as one of the University's worship assistants.

Alice Major

Alice Major is an award-winning poet and essayist (*Intersecting Sets: A Poet looks at Science*). Her twelfth book of poetry, *Knife on Snow*, has been described as "lyrical, expansive and incandescent." It's a volume that entwines her deep interest in science with the myths and narratives through which we try to make sense of our times and our vulnerable planet. Previous works have been recognized with awards such as the Pat Lowther Prize, the Malahat Long Poem prize and the Stephan G. Stephansson award. Recently she has been a contributor to "Reimagining Fire," a project to bring visual artists, writers, and scientists together to create work related to climate change, and was invited to read at the UN's COP15 conference on biodiversity in Montreal. She also founded the Edmonton Poetry Festival and has been chair of organizations such as the League of Canadian Poets, the Writers' Guild of Alberta, and the Edmonton Arts Council. She also served as the City of Edmonton's first poet laureate and has received the Lieutenant Governor of Alberta Distinguished Artist Award as well as an honorary doctorate from the University of Alberta. Her website is alicemajor.com.

Peter Mahaffy

Peter Mahaffy, FCIC, is a 3M national teaching fellow, professor of chemistry at The King's University in Edmonton, Canada, and director of The King's Centre for Visualization in Science (kcvs. ca), which provides digital learning resources used by a half-million students, educators, and the public from over one hundred countries each year. His current research and professional work is at the interfaces of chemistry education, systems thinking and sustainability, the uses of interactive visualization tools to facilitate the learning of science, and the responsible uses of chemistry. At an international level, he has contributed to and benefitted from collaborations with the International Union of Pure & Applied Chemistry (IUPAC), the International Council of Science, and the Organization for the Prohibition of Chemical Weapons. In working to tackle global challenges, he values and practices the convergence of disciplines that includes natural and social sciences, the humanities, and the arts.

His work has been recognized with national and international awards from the Chemical Institute of Canada, College Chemistry Canada, the American Chemical Society (ACS), and IUPAC. In March 2025, he received the ACS George C. Pimental Award for outstanding contributions to chemistry education.

Lori Matties

Lorraine Matties holds an undergraduate degree in English (University of Alberta), and a master's degree in biblical studies (Regent College). In her work as a trained spiritual director, she has encountered climate grief among her directees. Of late, she has served as the Creation Care Coordinator for her church, which is working to live into the creational mandate of stewarding the earth through education, gardening, and civic advocacy. She has published poems in several anthologies and journals.

Joanne M. Moyer

Joanne M. Moyer is an associate professor of environmental studies and geography and director of the environmental studies program at The King's University in Edmonton, Alberta. She received a PhD in natural resource and environmental management from the University of Manitoba, studying learning for sustainability in the context of faith-based organizations doing environmental and development work in Kenya. She then launched a research program investigating faith-based environmental engagement in Canada, with a recent focus on Mennonite environmental sustainability initiatives. She teaches courses such as Introduction to Sustainability, Simplicity and Consumption: Living Sustainably, Natural Resource Management, Human Geography, and The Global Village: Flourishing in an Interconnected World. She has worked with the Mennonite Central Committee and currently serves on the Sustainability Leadership Group for Mennonite Church Canada. Faith communities regularly ask Joanne to provide public education presentations on "creation care," a Christian approach to environmental sustainability. Joanne is also a community gardener and year-round commuter cyclist.

Justin Dodd Mullikin

Justin grew up on one of the last full-time tobacco farms in central Kentucky, USA, sparking a lifelong interest in agrarian change. Before completing a PhD in geography at Rutgers University, Justin worked in Rwanda for six years with an agrarian development NGO. His dissertation research on ambivalence and agrarian change in eastern Rwanda was motivated by the many questions, hopes, and expectations from farmers there that seemed to be ignored by mainstream development discourse and practice. Justin currently lives in Philadelphia where he is a lecturer in the critical writing program at the University of Pennsylvania.

David Rutherford

David Rutherford has been an assistant/associate professor in the multi-disciplinary Department of Public Policy Leadership at the University of Mississippi since 2006. He also directed the Mississippi Geographic Alliance for most of that time, working to improve the quantity and quality of geography in the schools of the state. His undergraduate and master's degrees were in geography, and he earned his PhD in geography/geographic education from Texas State University. His broad background in research and teaching in geography covers physical, human, regional, techniques, and educational components of the discipline with a focus on the world in which we live. David's teaching and research has been on major dynamics in the contemporary world. He has received various national teaching awards and published books, book chapters, journal articles, reports, artwork, and poetry, along with securing numerous grants and conducting many workshop and training sessions. For more information, visit David's website at davidrutherford.org.

Ashley Sakundiak

Ashley Sakundiak is a dedicated educator based in the Grande Prairie, Alberta, area. She was born and raised on an acreage near Vermilion, Alberta, where she and her three siblings spent their time raising a flock of purebred Hampshire sheep. As a family, they traveled across the province to compete in local agricultural shows, gaining valuable hands-on experience in showmanship, public speaking, and networking. A significant influence in Ashley's early life was her involvement in the 4-H program, which played a pivotal role in nurturing her passion for agriculture, leadership, communication, and youth mentoring. These formative experiences inspired her to pursue a career in education, where she could combine her love for working with youth and her background in rural life. Ashley holds a bachelor of arts degree in social sciences from The King's University and a bachelor's degree in education from the University of Alberta. Outside the classroom, Ashley enjoys spending time outdoors—whether it's camping, kayaking, or hiking—and is also passionate about sports, reading, and crafting. She brings enthusiasm, creativity, and a strong sense of community to everything she does, both professionally and personally.

Jane Satterfield

Jane Satterfield was born in Corby, England, to an American airman and a British mother. Her most recent books are *The Badass*

Brontës (a Diode Editions winner, 2023) and *Apocalypse Mix* (Autumn House Prize, 2017). Earlier books include *Her Familiars, Assignation at Vanishing Point* (Elixir Press Poetry Award), and *Shepherdess with an Automatic* (Towson University Prize). With Laurie Kruk, she co-edited the multi-genre anthology *Borderlands and Crossroads: Writing the Motherland.* A National Endowment for the Arts poetry fellow, Satterfield has received several Maryland Arts Council grants, while individual poems have won Bellingham Review's 49th Parallel Poetry Prize and awards from the Ledbury Festival and *Mslexia* magazine (both UK-based). She has received fellowships from the Arvon Foundation (UK), the Virginia Center for the Creative Arts, and Sewanee. Satterfield has served on the faculty of the West Chester Poetry Conference, the Frost Farm Conference, and as the 2019 Salisbury, Maryland Poet-in-Residence. She is married to poet Ned Balbo and lives in Baltimore, where she is a professor of writing at Loyola University Maryland. For more, visit janesatterfield.org.

Francesca Tronetti

Dr. Francesca Tronetti is the director of youth services at the Erie Multicultural Community Resource Center, where she oversees after-school programs for refugee and immigrant children in middle and high school. She is also an adjunct at Cherry Hill Seminary. She writes articles on ancient goddess cultures and contemporary American paganism for *Return to Mago* online magazine. She is interested in American folk magic traditions of Appalachia and the Pennsylvania Dutch and developed a course on the subject. A published poet, author, and fiber artist, she hosts a weekly community radio program on green living and self-care. She lives in Northwestern Pennsylvania and studies American mythological creatures and legends.

Cynthia Wallace

Cynthia R. Wallace is associate professor of English and the director of the Irene and Doug Schmeiser Centre for Faith, Reason, Peace, and Justice at St. Thomas More College, University of Saskatchewan, Canada. Her research and teaching focus on the intersections of contemporary literatures, religion, and philosophical ethics, and justice movements. Her creative and scholarly writing has appeared in *Contemporary Literature, Religion and Literature, Christianity and Literature, Arizona Quarterly, The Kenyon Review, The New England Review, Sojourners, Commonweal, The Christian Century*, and elsewhere. She is author of the books *Of Women Borne: A Literary Ethics of Suffering* (Columbia UP, 2016) and *The Literary Afterlives of Simone Weil: Feminism, Justice, and the Challenge of Religion* (Columbia UP, 2024) and shares occasional essays at AgonisticCommunion.substack.com.

Sarah Wallace

Sarah R. Wallace spent her formative years on Treaty 6 Territory, Canada, which features in her poem "Letter from Lake Barnett." She has studied English and creative writing at the University of New Brunswick and the University of Edinburgh, and she continues to research poetry, postsecularism, and pedagogy while working as an English instructor and writing center director. Sarah's poetry has been longlisted for the Mitchell Prize for Faith and Poetry, and she is currently working on a poetry chapbook that explores the book of Qohelet (Ecclesiastes) in relation to the Anthropocene.

Bibliography

Abram, David. *The Spell of the Sensuous: Perception and Language in a More-Than-Human World*. New York: Pantheon, 1996.

Albrecht, Glenn. *Earth Emotions: New Words for a New World*. Ithaca, NY: Cornell University Press, 2019.

———. "Solastalgia: A New Concept in Health and Identity." *Philosophy Activism Nature* 3 (2005) 44–59.

Augustine, Sarah. *The Land Is Not Empty: Following Jesus in Dismantling the Doctrine of Discovery*. Harrisonburg, VA: Harold, 2021.

Azoulay, Ariella. *The Civil Contract of Photography*. New York: Zone, 2008.

Balasundaram, Ranul, and Amali Tower. "Colombia Moves Closer to Officially Recognizing Internal Climate Displacement." Climate Refugees, May 30, 2023. https://www.climate-refugees.org/spotlight/2023/5/30-colombia.

Bate, Jonathan, and Paula Byrne, eds. *Stressed, Unstressed: Classic Poems to Ease the Mind*. London: HarperCollins, 2016.

BBC News. "Northern White Rhino: Last Male Sudan Dies in Kenya." Mar. 20, 2018. https://www.bbc.com/news/world-africa-43468066.

Berry, Thomas. *The Dream of the Earth*. San Francisco: Sierra Club, 1988.

Berry, Wendell. *Life Is a Miracle: An Essay Against Modern Superstition*. Berkeley, CA: Counterpoint, 2001.

———. *The Unsettling of America: Culture and Agriculture*. San Francisco: Sierra Club, 1977.

Biology Insights. "Environmental Impact of Dairy Farming: A Comprehensive Analysis." Apr. 29, 2025. https://biologyinsights.com/environmental-impact-of-dairy-farming-a-comprehensive-analysis/.

Braun, Connie. "Vigil for the Seven Children Who Died in Migrant Detainment Camps." In *Unspoken: An Inheritance of Words*. North Vancouver, BC: Alfred Gustav, 2020.

Brooks, Joanna, and Jay Clayton. *American Lazarus: Religion and the Rise of African-American and Native American Literatures*. New York: Oxford University Press, 2003.

Brueggemann, Walter. *Materiality as Resistance: Five Elements for Moral Action in the Real World*. Louisville: Westminster John Knox, 2020.

———. *The Prophetic Imagination*. 2nd ed. Minneapolis: Fortress, 2001.

———. *Reality, Grief, Hope: Three Urgent Prophetic Tasks*. Grand Rapids: Eerdmans, 2014.

Bryce, P. H. *The Story of a National Crime: Being an Appeal for Justice to the Indians of Canada*. Ottawa: James Hope & Sons, 1922.

Buber, Martin. *I and Thou*. Translated by Walter Kaufmann. New York: Scribner's Sons, 1970.

Burger, Ariel. *Witness: Lessons from Elie Wiesel's Classroom*. New York: Houghton Mifflin Harcourt, 2018.

Burke, Lauretta, et al. *Reefs at Risk Revisited*. Washington, DC: World Resources Institute, 2011.

Butler, William Francis. *The Great Lone Land: A Narrative of Travel and Adventure in the North-West of America*. London: Sampson Low, Marston, Low, & Searle, 1872.

California Department of Forestry and Fire Protection (CAL FIRE). "Tea Fire." Nov. 17, 2008. https://www.fire.ca.gov/incidents/2008/11/13/tea-fire/.

Cappiello, Julie. "Lolita: What Happened to the Orca Who Lived at Miami Seaquarium." World Animal Protection, June 21, 2024. https://www.worldanimalprotection.us/latest/blogs/lolita-what-happened-to-the-orca-who-lived-at-miami-seaquarium/.

Cecco, Leyland. "Canada Discovers 751 Unmarked Graves at Former Residential School." *Guardian*, June 24, 2021. https://www.theguardian.com/world/2021/jun/24/canada-school-graves-discovery-saskatchewan.

Childs, Craig. *Apocalyptic Planet: Field Guide to the Future of the Earth*. New York: Vintage, 2013.

Clark, Timothy. *The Cambridge Introduction to Literature and the Environment*. Cambridge: Cambridge University Press, 2011.

Cohen, Stanley. *States of Denial: Knowing About Atrocities and Suffering*. Cambridge: Polity, 2001.

Copeland, M. Shawn. *Enfleshing Freedom: Body, Race, and Being*. Minneapolis: Fortress, 2010.

Cowperthwaite, Gabriela, dir. *Blackfish*. New York: Magnolia Pictures, 2013.

Crutzen, Paul J. "Geology of Mankind." *Nature* 415.6867 (2002) 23. https://doi.org/10.1038/415023a.

Cunsolo, Ashlee, and Karen Landman, eds. *Mourning Nature: Hope at the Heart of Ecological Loss and Grief*. Montreal & Kingston: McGill-Queen's University Press, 2017.

Cunsolo, Ashlee, and Neville R. Ellis. "Ecological Grief as a Mental Health Response to Climate Change-Related Loss." *Nature Climate Change* 8.4 (2018) 275–81.

Dalley, Stephanie. *Myths from Mesopotamia: Creation, the Flood, Gilgamesh, and Others*. Oxford: Oxford University Press, 1989.

Daly, Natasha. "Orcas Don't Do Well in Captivity. Here's Why." *National Geographic*, March 25, 2019. https://www.nationalgeographic.com/animals/article/orcas-captivity-welfare.

Bibliography

Davenport, N. *Journal of a Fourteen Days' Ride Through the Bush from Quebec to Lake St. John.* Quebec: Daily Mercury Office, 1872. https://archive.org/details/cihm_02509/mode/2up.

deGaris, Lauri. "Tokitae: A Captive Orca Who Never Forgot Her Mother's Song." *Fernandina Observer,* Sept. 2, 2023. https://www.fernandinaobserver.org/stories/tokitae-a-captive-orca-who-never-forgot-her-mothers-song,16075.

DeFelicé, Mia. "10 Years After Crisis, Flint Is Still Fighting for Clean Water." Food & Water Watch, Apr. 25, 2024. https://www.foodandwaterwatch.org/2024/04/25/flint-10-years-later/.

Delcas, Marie. "La Niña and Global Warming Blamed as Torrential Rains Swamp Colombia." *Guardian,* May 10, 2011. https://www.theguardian.com/world/2011/may/10/heavy-rains-flooding-colombia.

Department of Justice Canada. "Aeronautics Act (RSC 1985, c. A–2)." https://laws-lois.justice.gc.ca/eng/acts/a-2/.

Dickinson, Emily. "Tell All the Truth but Tell It Slant—(1263)." Poetry Foundation. https://www.poetryfoundation.org/poems/56824/tell-all-the-truth-but-tell-it-slant-1263.

Dillard, Annie. *Holy the Firm.* New York: Harper & Row, 1977.

Douglas, Leah. "Trump Administration Cancels $3 Billion Climate-Friendly Farming Program." Successful Farming, Apr. 14, 2025. https://www.agriculture.com/trump-administration-cancels-usd3-billion-climate-friendly-farming-program-11715159.

Encyclopedia Britannica. "Psalms." Nov. 3, 2025. https://www.britannica.com/topic/biblical-literature/Psalms#ref597821.

Fields, Ashleigh. "Marjorie Taylor Greene: Federal Workers Don't Deserve Their Paychecks." *Hill,* Feb. 26, 2025. https://thehill.com/homenews/house/5165176-marjorie-taylor-greene-criticized/.

Ferber, Michael P., and Randolph Haluza-DeLay. "Scale-Jumping and Climate Change in the Geography of Religion." In *The Changing World Religion Map: Sacred Places, Identities, Practices and Politics,* edited by Stanley D. Brunn, 193–210. Dordrecht, NL: Springer, 2015. https://doi.org/10.1007/978-94-017-9376-6_10.

Garrard, Greg. *Ecocriticism.* 3rd ed. London: Routledge, 2023.

Gilchrist, Emma. "What Our Grief for Jasper Tells Us About Our Love for the Natural World." Narwhal, July 26, 2024. https://thenarwhal.ca/jasper-fire-grief/.

Glavin, Terry. "Canada Slowly Acknowledging There Never Was a 'Mass Grave.'" *National Post,* May 30, 2024. https://nationalpost.com/opinion/terry-glavin-canada-slowly-acknowledging-there-never-was-a-mass-grave.

Golding, Barry, and Annette Foley. "Constructing Narratives in Later Life: Autoethnography Beyond the Academy." *Australian Journal of Adult Learning* 57.3 (2017) 384–400. https://files.eric.ed.gov/fulltext/EJ1164157.pdf.

Goldman, Jason G. "Bird Song Became Softer During the Pandemic Thanks to Less Noise Pollution." *Audubon Magazine*, Spring 2021. https://www.audubon.org/magazine/spring-2021/bird-song-became-softer-during-pandemic-thanks.

Goring, Ruth. *Dearworthy: Little Meditations on the Revelations of Julian of Norwich*. Chicago: Paraclete, 2024.

———. *Picturing God*. Minneapolis: Beaming, 2019.

Goring, Ruth, and Michael Bracey. *Caras lindas de Colombia* [Beautiful faces of Colombia]. Chicago: Catalyst Zone, 2018.

Goring Stewart, Ruth. *Environmental Stewardship: 8 Studies for Individuals or Groups*. Global Issues Bible Studies. Downers Grove, IL: InterVarsity, 1990.

Flanagan, Tom. "Murray Sinclair's Fabrications." *Dorchester Review*, Oct. 4, 2021.

Francis, Pope. *Laudato Si': On Care for Our Common Home*. Vatican City: Libreria Editrice Vaticana, 2015.

Frye, Northrop. *The Bush Garden: Essays on the Canadian Imagination*. Toronto: Anansi, 1971.

Hatch, Edwin. "Breathe on Me, Breath of God." In *Between Doubt and Prayer*. London: Macmillan, 1878.

Hoagland, Tony. "Peaceful Transition." *New Yorker*, Nov. 5, 2018. https://www.newyorker.com/magazine/2018/11/05/peaceful-transition.

———. *Unincorporated Persons in the Late Honda Dynasty: Poems*. Minneapolis: Graywolf, 2010.

Hoffman, Andrew J. *Business School and the Noble Purpose of the Market: Correcting the Systemic Failures of Shareholder Capitalism*. Stanford, CA: Stanford Business, 2025.

hooks, bell. *Belonging: A Culture of Place*. New York: Routledge, 2019.

Hopkins, Gerard Manley. "God's Grandeur." Poetry Foundation. https://www.poetryfoundation.org/poems/44395/gods-grandeur.

Hoyos, N., et al. "Impact of the 2010–2011 La Niña Phenomenon in Colombia, South America: The Human Toll of an Extreme Weather Event." *Applied Geography* 39 (May 2013) 16–25. https://www.sciencedirect.com/science/article/abs/pii/S0143622812001610.

Hübl, Thomas. "The Anatomy of Inaction: Climate Change and Collective Trauma, Day 3 PP@COP26." Pocket Project, Nov. 3, 2021. https://www.youtube.com/watch?v=VF9j5uktTUk.

Ivory, Karen. "Murdered by What Was in the Air: The Donora Smog Crisis 1948." In *Pennsylvania Disasters: True Stories of Tragedy and Survival*. Essex, CT: Globe Pequot, 2015.

Janik, Del Ivan. "Environmental Consciousness in Modern Literature: Four Representative Examples." In *Deep Ecology for the Twenty-first Century: Reading on the Philosophy and Practice of the New Environmentalism*, edited by George Sessions, 131–48. Boston: Shambhala, 1995.

Jennings, Willie James. *Can "White" People Be Saved? Triangulating Race, Theology, and Mission.* Downers Grove, IL: InterVarsity, 2018.

———. *The Christian Imagination: Theology and the Origins of Race.* New Haven, CT: Yale University Press, 2010.

Kent, Aaron, and Charlie Baylis, eds. *Footprints: An Anthology of New Ecopoetry.* Llandysul, UK: Broken Sleep, 2022.

Kimmerer, Robin Wall. *Braiding Sweetgrass: Indigenous Wisdom, Scientific Knowledge, and the Teachings of Plants.* Minneapolis: Milkweed, 2013.

Kincaid, Jamaica. *A Small Place.* New York: Farrar, Straus and Giroux, 1988.

Kipling, Rudyard. *The Collected Poems of Rudyard Kipling.* London: Wordsworth, 1994.

Klein, Naomi. *This Changes Everything: Capitalism vs. the Climate.* New York: Simon & Schuster, 2014.

Knox, Paul L. "World Cities and the Organization of Global Space." In *Geographies of Global Change,* edited by R. J. Johnston et al., 328–39. Oxford: Blackwell, 1995.

Kohn, Eduardo. *How Forests Think: Toward an Anthropology Beyond the Human.* Berkeley: University of California Press, 2013.

Kolbert, Elizabeth. "Climate Change from A to Z." *New Yorker,* Nov. 21, 2022.

Lakhani, Nina. "Emissions from Israel's War in Gaza Have 'Immense' Effect on Climate Catastrophe." *Guardian,* Jan. 9, 2024. https://www.theguardian.com/world/2024/jan/09/emissions-gaza-israel-hamas-war-climate-change.

Larsen, Karin. "Airspace over Former Kamloops Indian Residential School Restricted." CBC News, June 4, 2021. https://www.cbc.ca/news/canada/british-columbia/airspace-restricted-over-former-kamloops-indian-residential-school-1.6054265.

Liester, Mitchell B. "When Cell Phones Replace People." *Psychology Today,* May 7, 2025. https://www.psychologytoday.com/ca/blog/the-leading-edge/202505/when-cell-phones-replace-people.

Lindeman, Tracey. "Canada: Remains of 215 Children Found at Indigenous Residential School Site." *Guardian,* May 28, 2021. https://www.theguardian.com/world/2021/may/28/canada-remains-indigenous-children-mass-graves.

Lowenthal, David. "Revisiting Valued Landscapes." In *Valued Environments,* edited by John R. Gold and Jacquelin Burgess, 88–90. London: George Allen & Unwin, 1982.

Macfarlane, Robert. *Underland: A Deep Time Journey.* New York: Norton, 2020.

Machado, Antonio. "Proverbios y cantares." Section 29 in *Campos de Castilla.* Barcelona: Ediciones La Flámula, 2022. https://archive.org/details/antonio-machado.-campos-de-castilla/page/n105/mode/2up.

Malcolm, Hannah, ed. *Words for a Dying World: Stories of Grief and Courage from the Global Church.* London: SCM, 2020.

Malisch, Sherrie. "In Praise of the Garrison Mentality: Why Fear and Retreat May Be Useful Responses in an Era of Climate Change." *Studies in Canadian Literature* 39.1 (2014) 177–98.

Maynard, Robyn, and Leanne Betasamosake Simpson. *Rehearsals for Living*. Toronto: Alfred A. Knopf Canada, 2022.

McDermott, Jennifer. "Trump Administration Cancels Clean Energy Grants as It Prioritizes Fossil Fuels." *Associated Press*, Mar. 28, 2025. https://apnews.com/article/trump-energy-department-clean-energy-wind-solar-batteries-hydrogen-fossil-fuels-cf1dff9ee771c566765e9ca3e3599d91.

McDuff, Mallory. *Love Your Mother: 50 States, 50 Stories, and 50 Women United for Climate Justice*. Glasgow: Broadleaf, 2023.

Mendoza, Luis Felipe. "Colombia: Climate Change Drives Forced Displacement." *Colombia One*, Apr. 26, 2024. https://colombiaone.com/2024/04/26/colombia-climate-change-displacement/.

Metres, Philip. "Beyond Grief and Grievance: The Poetry of 9/11 and Its Aftermath." Poetry Foundation, June 15, 2022. https://www.poetryfoundation.org/articles/69737/beyond-grief-and-grievance.

Moe-Lobeda, Cynthia D. *Resisting Structural Evil: Love as Ecological-Economic Vocation*. Minneapolis: Fortress, 2013.

Moodie, Susanna. *Roughing It in the Bush*. Toronto: Ryerson University, 2022. https://pressbooks.library.torontomu.ca/roughingitinthebush/.

Moore, Marianne. "Poetry." In *Others for 1919: An Anthology of the New Verse*, edited by Alfred Kreymborg. New York: N. L. Brown, 1920.

Myers, Ched. *Binding the Strong Man: A Political Reading of Mark's Story of Jesus*. 20th anniversary ed. Maryknoll, NY: Orbis, 2008.

National Archives of Canada. "Department of Indian Affairs and Northern Development Fonds (Record Group 10). Vol. 6810, file 470-72-3, vols. 7, 55 (L-3), and 63 (N-3)." Library and Archives Canada (LAC), Ottawa.

National Centre for Truth and Reconciliation. "Residential School History." https://nctr.ca/education/teaching-resources/residential-school-history/.

National Oceanic and Atmospheric Administration (NOAA). "Ocean Acidification." Sept. 25, 2025. https://www.noaa.gov/education/resource-collections/ocean-coasts/ocean-acidification.

Natural Resources Canada. "National Wildland and Fire Situation Report." Sept. 8, 2021. https://natural-resources.canada.ca/stories/simply-science/canadas-record-breaking-wildfires-2023-fiery-wake-call.

Nemeth, Erwin, et al. "Clamorous City Blackbirds: Birds Can Sing Louder at Higher Frequencies and Thereby Make Themselves Heard in Traffic Noise." Max Planck Society, Jan. 11, 2013. https://www.mpg.de/6814595/city-blackbirds-traffic-noise.

NOAA Fisheries. "Southern Resident Killer Whale (Orcinus Orca)." Feb. 5, 2024. https://www.fisheries.noaa.gov/west-coast/endangered-species-conservation/southern-resident-killer-whale-orcinus-orca.

NOAA National Centers for Environmental Information. "Ocean Acidification." July 19, 2024. https://www.ncei.noaa.gov/news/quantifying-ocean-carbon-sink.

Orca Network. "The Capture." https://www.orcanetwork.org/tokitaesstory/blog-post-title-two-6scey.

———. "Tokitae's Life Now." https://www.orcanetwork.org/tokitaesstory/blog-post-title-three-tslkw.

Oxford English Dictionary. 3rd ed. Oxford: Oxford University Press, 2025. https://www.oed.com.

Plumwood, Val. *Environmental Culture: The Ecological Crisis of Reason.* London: Routledge, 2002.

Prairie Climate Centre. *A Snapshot of the Changing Prairie Climate.* ClimateWest, June 14, 2023. https://climatewest.ca/wp-content/uploads/2023/06/Snapshot-Changing_Prairie-Climate-2022.pdf.

Pratt, Mary Louise. *Imperial Eyes: Travel Writing and Transculturation.* London: Routledge, 2008.

Prior, Tim, and Christine Eriksen. "Wildfire Preparedness, Community Cohesion and Social-Ecological Systems." *Global Environmental Change* 23.6 (2013) 1575–86. https://doi.org/10.1016/j.gloenvcha.2013.09.016.

Pulido, Laura. "Geographies of Race and Ethnicity I: White Supremacy vs. White Privilege in Environmental Racism Research." *Progress in Human Geography* 39.6 (2015) 809–17.

Purdue Global Law School. "Corporate Personhood: What It Means and How It Has Evolved." Jan. 6, 2023. https://www.purduegloballawschool.edu/blog/news/corporate-personhood.

Rah, Soong-Chan. *Prophetic Lament: A Call for Justice in Troubled Times.* Downers Grove, IL: InterVarsity, 2015.

Rauer, Valentin. "Symbols in Action: Willy Brandt's Kneefall at the Warsaw Memorial." In *Social Performance: Symbolic Action, Cultural Pragmatics, and Ritual,* edited by Jeffrey C. Alexander, et al., 257–82. Cambridge: Cambridge University Press, 2006.

Relph, Edward. *Place and Placelessness.* London: Pion, 1976.

Ross, Shawna. *Charlotte Brontë at the Anthropocene.* Albany, NY: SUNY, 2020.

Said, Edward W. *Orientalism.* New York: Pantheon, 1978.

Satterfield, Jane. *The Badass Brontës.* Richmond, VA: Diode, 2023.

———. "Endling." Poets Reading the News, Mar. 20, 2018. https://www.poetsreadingthenews.com/2018/03/endling-jane-satterfield-poetry/.

Scranton, Roy. *Learning to Die in the Anthropocene: Reflections on the End of a Civilization.* San Francisco: City Lights, 2015.

Shelley, Percy. "A Defence of Poetry." Poetry Foundation, Mar. 13, 2020. https://www.poetryfoundation.org/articles/69388/a-defence-of-poetry.

Shklovsky, Viktor. "Art, as Device." *Poetics Today* 36.3 (2015) 151–74. https://doi.org/10.1215/03335372-3160709.

Simard, Suzanne. *Finding the Mother Tree: Discovering the Wisdom of the Forest.* New York: Knopf, 2021.

Sinclair, Murray. "Statement on Residential School Burial Sites." Indian Residential School History and Dialogue Centre, University of British Columbia, June 1, 2021. https://irshdc.ubc.ca/2021/06/04/murray-sinclair/.

Singh, Neera M. "The Affective Labor of Growing Forests and the Becoming of Environmental Subjects: Rethinking Environmentality in Odisha, India." *Geoforum* 47 (2013) 189–98. https://doi.org/10.1016/j.geoforum.2013.01.010.

Solnit, Rebecca. "Slow Change Can Be Radical Change." Literary Hub, Jan. 11, 2024. https://lithub.com/rebecca-solnit-slow-change-can-be-radical-change/.

Sontag, Susan. *Regarding the Pain of Others.* New York: Farrar, Straus and Giroux, 2003.

Sorkin, Michael. "Introduction: Variations on a Theme Park." In *Variations on a Theme Park: Scenes from the New American City and the End of Public Space,* edited by Michael Sorkin, xi–xv. New York: Hill and Wang, 1992.

Spry, Tami. *Body, Paper, Stage: Writing and Performing Autoethnography.* New York: Routledge, 2011.

———. "Performing Autoethnography: An Embodied Methodological Praxis." *Qualitative Inquiry* 7.6 (2002) 706–32. https://doi.org/10.1177/107780040100700605.

Stewart, Ruth Goring. *Environmental Stewardship.* Downers Grove, IL: InterVarsity, 1990.

Stockholm Resilience Centre. "Planetary Boundaries." https://www.stockholmresilience.org/research/planetary-boundaries/the-nine-planetary-boundaries.html.

Stroebe, Margaret. "The Poetry of Grief: Beyond Scientific Portrayal." *OMEGA–Journal of Death and Dying* 78 (2018) 67–96. https://doi.org/10.1177/0030222818792706.

Subramanian, Petar M. V., et al. "Global Quieting of High-Frequency Seismic Noise Due to COVID-19 Pandemic Lockdown Measures." *Science* 369.6509 (2020) 1338–43. https://doi.org/10.1126/science.abd2438.

Tk'emlúps te Secwépemc. "Office of the Chief for Immediate Release." May 27, 2021. https://web.archive.org/web/20250110142736/https://tkemlups.ca/wp-content/uploads/05-May-27-2021-TteS-MEDIA-RELEASE.pdf.

Tuan, Yi-Fu. *Topophilia: A Study of Environmental Perception, Attitudes, and Values.* New York: Columbia University Press, 1990.

Tuck, Eve, and K. Wayne Yang. "Decolonization Is Not a Metaphor." *Decolonization: Indigeneity, Education & Society* 1.1 (2012) 1–40.

Tyndale, William. *The New Testament Translated by William Tyndale 1534.* Edited by David Daniell. New Haven, CT: Yale University Press, 1989.

The Unthanks. "The Unthanks—Lines—Part Three—Emily Bronte." Mar. 14, 2022. https://www.youtube.com/watch?v=db9VTAHN7S8.

Vitale, Ami. "What I Learned Documenting the Last Male Northern White Rhino's Death." *National Geographic,* Aug. 2019. https://www.

nationalgeographic.com/animals/article/life-changing-lessons-of-the-last-male-northern-white-rhino.

Wallace-Wells, David. *The Uninhabitable Earth: Life After Warming*. New York: Tim Duggan, 2019.

Walsh, Brian J., and J. Richard Middleton. *The Transforming Vision: Shaping a Christian World View*. Downers Grove, IL: InterVarsity, 1984.

White, Lynn, Jr. "The Historical Roots of Our Ecologic Crisis." *Science* 155.3767 (1967) 1203–7.

Woolf, Virginia. *The Common Reader*. Project Gutenberg. https://www.gutenberg.org/files/64457/64457-h/64457-h.html.

World Bank. "Green Your Bus Ride: Clean Buses in Latin America." Jan. 2019. https://documents1.worldbank.org/curated/en/410331548180859451/pdf/133929-WP-PUBLIC-P164403-Summary-Report-Green-Your-Bus-Ride.pdf.

WorldOMeter. "Colombia Demographics." https://www.worldometers.info/demographics/colombia-demographics/.

Wright, Christopher J. H. *The Message of Lamentations: Honest to God*. Downers Grove, IL: IVP Academic, 2015.

Wynter, Sylvia. "Novel and History, Plot and Plantation." *Savacou* 1.5 (1971) 95–102.

Xiang, David Haosen, and Alisha Moon Yi. "A Look Back and a Path Forward: Poetry's Healing Power During the Pandemic." *Journal of Medical Humanities* 41.4 (Dec. 2020) 603–8.

www.ingramcontent.com/pod-product-compliance
Lightning Source LLC
Chambersburg PA
CBHW061733270326
41928CB00011B/2217